# The Life of Eli and Amanda
## Founders of Yoder's, Inc.

Yoder's Locker Plant buildings in the early 1960s.

Cover photo: Eli and Amanda in front of their home

Printed at Mennonite Publishing House,
Scottdale, Pennsylvania 1992

# Contents

# Preface

My first recollection of the Eli Yoder family goes back to my childhood when they ate Sunday dinner at our house. The outstanding impression was the cute, sweet, little baby girl, Mabel, they had. At that time not even the oldest son impressed me. Indeed, I cannot recall that there were any boys.

That evening when my nieces (my brother Noah's daughters) and I met on the coal hills close to Noah's home, we had a heated argument about which baby was cutest, Eli Yoder's Mabel who was at our house or Ezra Yoder's Frieda, who had a pretty pink dress on and was at Noah's for dinner.

Later on the Yoder's became better known to me through Tillie Wengerd who worked for them and later married my brother Irvin Beachy. Tillie was somewhat like one of their family and since I often traveled with Irvin's I was a frequent guest there. As time went on the daughters matured and were good friends of mine. Eventually the Lord led the oldest son, Henry, and I together and I became one of the family.

In 1967 when their 50th wedding anniversary was coming up the family asked me to compile a "This Is Your Life" to be read at their anniversary supper. Dad and Mother, unaware of the plans, cooperated beautifully, supplying stories and information from the past.

Over the years the sincere Christian principles, integrity in business deals, steadfast faith, kindness, and help bestowed on their family have been a challenge to me. My involvement in caring for my mother-in-law after she had a stroke in 1976 drew the relationship with both Mother and Dad very close, showering me with innumerable blessings.

The Lord granted Dad and Mother 16 years of life after the compilation of "This Is Your Life." As time went on after their passing, Dad on January 5, 1983, and Mother on May 29, 1983, I was impressed with the thought that there would be many great grandchildren who never had the privilege of knowing Dad and Mother and it seemed their life story should be in print for future generations. From this line of thought came the inspiration to bring "This Is Your Life" up-to-date, attempting to cover the highlights of their later experiences and activities, as well as their declining years.

Suffice it to say the task turned out to be greater than I anticipated and the finished product leaves discouragingly much to be desired.

4

Nevertheless, searching through old letters, ledgers, and notebooks for material was not only interesting and enjoyable, but challenging. Throughout the story, I have frequently used Pennsylvania German quotes. There is no Pennsylvania German dictionary for the dialect spoken in the Casselman Valley. Also there is a wide variation in usage and pronunciation of words from family to family. For example, my Beachy family was amused when Eli Tice's were our neighbors to hear Eli's wife, Mary, use the word "commons" for we said "fa common." Coming into Henry's family I found they also said "Commons" for Mary and Dad were both Lewis Yoder's offspring. To German scholars my Pennsylvania German spelling may seem inconsistent for rather than attempting to follow rules for German spelling I have attempted to spell Pennsylvania German words as they sound to me.

Ordinarily I avoid writing in first person, especially the use of the pronoun "I." However, with my close involvement in some instances it was too difficult to eliminate its use. As a general rule the first person pronouns I, or me, which are not in quotes (direct quotes of persons speaking themselves), refer to the author, Mary Elizabeth Yoder.

Copies of letters, notes, records, diaries, etc., are printed verbatim, spelling, punctuation, and capitalization as the originals.

--Mary Elizabeth Yoder (August 1991)

## Acknowledgement

To my loving husband and family without whose love and encouragement this story would not have been written.

Thanks to members of Eli and Amanda's family who shared their memories of the past and John and Grace Yoder who provided most of the family photos. Also, thanks to my son Eli Moses who took the October 1975 photo of Eli and Amanda on their porch and my nephew Philip Beachy who took the Christmas 1976 family photo.

Special thanks to my son Joseph who introduced me to the wonders of a computer and his wife, Mandy, who with her expertise taught me the basics of operating a computer, rescued me when I got "stuck," spent hours correcting goofs, editing and laying out the manuscript ready for "camera copy."

# The Eli L. Yoder Family

Eli Yoder was born to Lewis and Elizabeth (Lizzie) Yoder, May 27, 1896. The Yoder's lived on the Jacob Folk farm at the Maryland end of the Posey Row road. Three-and-a-half-year-old Clarence and two-year-old Amelia welcomed their little brother. Apparently theirs were not common Amish names for Lizzie said, "Des sol molh enn Amisher naumma hava," (This one shall have an Amish name once) and they used the Pennsylvania German form "Eally" rather than the English form Eli for the little boy.

As little boys, Eli and Clarence enjoyed fishing but it was forbidden in the absence of their parents. One day when Lewis's were away the boys disobeyed this rule, got their pole and took it down to the pond. Obviously feeling guilty they tried to keep behind the brush and cast their line across a stump. Soon they thought their line was caught. All their efforts to get it out failed and they had to call on Ben Butler, the hired hand, to help. Ben succeeded, not by loosening the line but by pulling out a large carp. The fish was loaded with eggs and the boys were so excited they wanted to go fishing again but their parents came home before they got to it. Both Eli and Clarence remembered this incident but neither of them recalled having been punished for their disobedience.

Then there was the occasion when Eli, already a budding gardener planted some beans. As he checked them over they appeared to have come up upside down. So he pulled them out and carefully replanted them. He did not recall whether they thrived after that experience.

In later years Eli reminisced about his childhood in the Lewis Yoder family letter. He kept all of the sheets of his family letters . Following are quotes from his May 12, 1957 sheet:

*"Yes I also remember how Dad and Mom used to be working, working out in the hot sun, came in all sweated up and about all in. When they cleared off a field it sure did cost a lot of sweat and hard work too. And there were still a lot of stumps on, where they just plowed around them and Dad would cradle the wheat by hand. He had a handkerchief hanging at him to wipe the sweat and was soaked all over too. Yes, then in the winter he used to haul props or cross ties to make (financial) ends meet. He had old Daise and Nell and a sled, and in all kinds of weather and used to drive his team to Frostburg with butter, eggs strawberries, dressed hogs or whatever they had, and over the rough old pike. Dad was raising coalts too. I think he*

*took the coalt along part ways, maybe as far as the Johnson farm. That trip took a good long day and part of the night. I also remember the ditch he dug to find coal, the further in the deeper. They found coal and found a mine. All this work was by hand, no tractor, buldozer, highlift or truck. After mine was finished coal were all hauled by teams waiting their turn for coal, (during winter) a lot of working and scratching to feed his hungry kids. There was always plenty provided for us. But I remember how good them fried potatoes were. At one time potatoes were rather scarce then when they had again I told Mom to fry six dishes full. Dads also boiled sugar and raised sheep and Durock hogs and besides that he always loved pets. He built a big cage where he had three coons. Somebody else write a big sheet full. "*

His next sheet dated August 4, 1957 continued his reminiscence. Referring to their fishing venture he says,

*"We had orders not to go fishing, because Mom was afraid we might fall in the dam. I suppose it would have been worse to fall in the dam than in the sugar barrel. Yes, Dads got a barrel of sugar at a time when they were about empty the little boys had quite a time to reach the sugar and one had a reck." (Notice he avoids naming the unfortunate boy.) " The cooky jar was not so bad. Sometimes the cooky jar was moved to another place, but the boys soon knew where it was. Yes candy and bananas were also wonderful. Them days you could buy three bananas for five cents. Clarence and I used to walk to Grantsville to get the mail and some other things and often we got a five cent box of peanuts which we ate going home. Them days we went barefooted. I remember some frosty mornings we would chase the cows up and stand on the warm spot to warm our feet. That was when the grass was white with frost and we fetched the cows in. Yes, I remember too how we laughed when Uncle Harvey upset the hand wagon. I may have a joke on myself the next time, "*
*(In telling about the sugar barrel he admitted that it was Eli who had the "reck," he fell into the barrel head first!) Eli related how his father showed him how to put butter into the syrup if it wanted to run over and then left him in charge of the sugar camp while he went to gather more sap. Sure enough the syrup threatened to run over. Eli, who was but a little boy quickly added butter but the syrup did not go down! So he ran to the door of the camp and shouted "Pap, Ich hopp bauch vay!" (Dad I have belly ache!)*

7

# Eli's Early School Days

Eli started to Shade Run School with serious misgivings because his brother Clarence had informed him that the teacher would paddle him. One day something happened that upset him and he ran outside crying. While the teacher was outside trying to coax him to come in, Sam Hershberger drove by. Eli said, "I guess he didn't think of it that the little boy out there crying would be his daughter's husband some day."

Eli's brother Simon related an incident when their father had assigned some jobs to the boys before leaving home. When Lewis came home and found one son's job undone he punished him. Later Lewis heard the boys who had done their work teasing the one who had received the punishment. "Ich guun dears yusht, Ich guun dears yusht. Siss yusht gut fer dich!"(Sickie on you, sickie on you. It's just good for you!) Lewis promptly squelched the teasing and punished the teasers as well. Since Eli did not recall the incident he concluded that he was not involved. He admitted that he may have needed "shlake" (a whipping) sometimes but could not remember ever having been spanked.

While working in the fields with his father on the Folk farm, Eli remembered seeing a strange looking thing coming down Route 40. When it came closer they saw that it was one of these new fangled automobiles that traveled without a horse. The excited onlookers watched until it was out of sight.

## The Family Moves to Niverton

In the spring of 1909 Lewis and Lizzie bought what is now the Simon C. Yoder farm from Lizzie's widowed mother, Mrs. Christian Beachy, and moved there. By this time Savilla, Amanda, Simon, Henry, Mary and Menno had joined the family and Eli was an energetic lad going on thirteen-years-old.

Three more children, Anna, Sarah, and Norman, were born after their move to Niverton. Anna died of spinal meningitis at the age of ten months. In one of Eli's family letter sheets he referred to her death. "Yes I remember how sick little Anna was and how she suffered and cried out so that I guess we all sort of wished she could die. We boys went out to the stable one morning to do the chores. While we were milking Mom came out to the stable and told us that our little sister had died and was no longer suffering. I think Mom was glad that she was relieved of her suffering."

8

After their move the Yoder children went to Cross Roads School. Eli did not get along too well with the Miller boys. One day he told Hubert Miller "All that the Millers are good for is to talk." This made Hubert's older brother angry and he threw a real hard snow ball into Eli's face. At the time Eli did not think he deserved that. But later on he concluded that maybe he did.

At the time of Sarah's birth in 1912 the family including Lewis had the measles. My Uncle Simon S. Miller (Gramp) with his gift of caring for the sick came to the rescue, took charge and nursed them back to health. One night when he was keeping close watch on delirious Eli, Eli shook the covers vigorously. "What are you doing?" asked Gramp. "Ich been molh om die radle doe raus shiddle!" replied Eli. (I'm shaking the measles out of here once!)

During this time it was unthinkable for a mother to get out of bed before her baby was ten days old. After the measles were all over Lewis told Lizzie, "Ich been dir sheer gore dote gonga und du bisht nett even cumma mich saena." (I almost died for you and you didn't even come to see me.) Lewis had been very sick but undoubtedly Lizzie would have been expected to die or at least suffer dire consequences if she had ventured out of bed before the tenth day!

## Eli's Youthful Business Ventures

Eli's eye for business and his determination to accomplish his goals showed up early in life. Of course his main job was helping his father and brothers on the farm, but there is also a notebook with careful records of his business transactions from 1910 to 1914 (age 14 to 17) depicting him as an ambitious youngster who did trapping and also raised chickens. Among expenses were, hatching eggs, 7 clucks @ 60¢, the use of 9 clucks @ 10¢, (results of his incubation were 93 peepies from 123 eggs). Other expenses were 1 trap @ 5¢ some things from the store for 3¢, 1 watch for 17¢, and postals for 2¢. Entered as income are eggs; chickens and roosters sold; 100 lbs. iron for 35¢, 1 mink hide for $3.00; a skunk hide for 10¢, 1 rat caught for 2¢, some hides (a cat and a calf) for 30¢, 8¢ for catching rats and for January 15, 1911, 25¢ for taking the buggy home! Larger amounts were 5 chickens at 55¢ a piece....$2.75 and 2 rosters breeder....$1.75 (supposedly breeder roosters).

Florence Yoder, a resident of Goodwill Mennonite Home, remembered Eli (a former pupil of hers) as an enterprising young salesman of Cloverine Salve and floor mops. Her father, Emanuel Yoder, invariably sent salesmen of household items to deal with his wife.

However he listened politely to Eli's sales talk.

Eli said, "They say the mops make the floors just as clean as you get them by getting down on your knees to scrub. But they don't." His straight-forward honesty so impressed Mr. Yoder that he bought a mop on the spot.

Milton E. Bender stated that he used to observe Eli Yoder in his boyhood and wondered what he would do some day. He was sure that Eli would make something of himself because he was always busy and not afraid to tackle things. But Milt didn't think of it that he would someday build a Locker Plant!

Eli matured into a handsome young man with dark hair, friendly hazel eyes and a hearty laugh. He was of moderate stature and rather slow motioned. In his youth he accepted Christ as his Savior and was baptized in the Amish church where he became acquainted with a fine Christian young woman with sparkling brown eyes and dark hair.

## Mandy Hershberger Appears on the Scene

Samuel and Elizabeth Tice Hershberger's 1897 Ledger lists as expense for January 15,1897: "Dr. Lichti by work, $8.00," this was the delivery fee for their first child, Amanda!

Tillie Tice Yoder remembered what thrilling news the arrival of this baby girl, her little cousin, was. Later Tillie went to her Aunt Lizzie's house to be "Kins maut" (nurse maid) for little Mandy. One day she was reading something on a cornstarch box and let the baby fall. Tillie felt terrible. Her aunt took the crying baby and remarked that Tillie probably would not be reading again when she was supposed to be watching the baby.

Baby Mandy fell asleep then, and Lizzie put her to bed. Tillie was afraid she might not wake up again and went into the bedroom over and over to check on her. Oh, how relieved she was when the baby woke up and seemed quite all right.

As a little girl Mandy liked to sit on the cellar steps and watch the hired girl, Mandy Tice, (later Mrs. Noah M. Yoder) do the churning.

In October of 1898 a little brother John arrived to be Mandy's playmate and in May 1900 a sister Effie, joined the family. In 1911 when Sam's parents, Emanuel Herhsberger's, took a trip west, Sam and Lizzie asked them to bring a baby from a children's home in Iowa along home for them whom they wished to adopt. The Iowa home was in the middle of an epidemic of some contagious disease at the time so arrangements were made and they went to another home to choose a baby. Tiny red-haired baby, Anna Francis Burton, between five and six months-old and weighing only eight and one-half pounds thrived on the Hershberger family's tender loving care. She matured to become Mrs. Calvin Baker and is now a widow. The story as related by her is when Grandpa Emanuel Hershberger's walked into a room of babies all but one of them was fussing. He walked over and spoke to her and she gave him a big friendly smile. So he chose the tiny little girl with red hair, blue eyes, and a big smile, and they brought her along home from Iowa by train. Three years later Barbara was born to complete the Hershberger family.

Dainty, little Mandy was always very quick motioned. Her father remarked that Mandy could run around her more slow motioned brother John three times before he got up when the children were playing on the floor.

## Mandy's School Days

When Mandy was six-years-old she stayed at Noah M. Yoder's, who lived where Herman Yoder's now live, so that she would not have so far to walk to what was then known as Dutch College School (later Yoder School). She remembered wearing felt boots to school. Although she did not get to go home for a period of nine weeks during bad weather she did not recall having been homesick. At the age of ten when she was at Noah's as "Kin's Maut" (child caring for younger children to help out when a new baby was born) she was homesick and usually shed tears in the evening.

One morning when Mandy was on her way to school she came to a place where snow had melted. There was water, ice and snow to cross which looked dangerous to her. She called for help and Amelia Miller (later Mrs. Alvin C. Schrock) came out and helped her across, then she went on to school. Alvin J. Miller who was Mandy's third grade teacher described her as a very pretty little girl and a good student. Mandy liked to walk to school with Lucy Miller Swartzentruber because meeting a "bohunk" (the name attached to the Italian miners from Niverton, Pa.) was not so frightening in her company as it was when she was alone.

Salome Bender Peachey worked for the Hershberger's when Mandy was a girl. Mandy's first recollection of having seen a photograph of an Amish person was a snapshot of Salome which she thought was very beautiful.

# Mandy Matures and Shoulders Responsibilities

When Mandy was fourteen-years-old her mother fell out of a cherry tree and hurt her back. The men who were building a cistern up on the hill helped to carry her into the house on a cot. While Lizzie was recuperating from her fall, Mandy took charge and with the help of others carried on the work; milking, separating, churning, washing, ironing, cooking and canning as well as caring for baby Anna who was just big enough to be propped in a sitting position with pillows at that time.

A postal card from her mother on her 15th birthday commends Mandy for the way she was taking care of her duties and expresses Lizzie's hope that she is doing just as well spiritually.

Although Mandy remained short (4' 10") and rather plump, she was very attractive with dark hair and expressive, friendly, brown eyes. She was also energetic, quick and efficient, all qualities which Eli admired. In her early teens she accepted Christ as her Saviour, took instructions and was baptized in the Amish church where she became acquainted with Eli.

## Youthful Activities

Old cards and letters reveal that Eli and Mandy occasionally went to the Summit Mills settlement to visit relatives on in-between weekends when there was no church service. At that time Church was held every other Sunday, one Sunday in the Summit Mills meeting house, known as the lower settlement and two weeks later in the Flag Run or Niverton meeting house, known as the upper settlement. On non-church Sundays people occasionally went visiting for a weekend, staying with friends Saturday night, making calls and having dinner and supper with more friends on Sunday. Letters also verify the fact that the Lewis Yoder and Moses Beachy families' youngsters were together a lot. I (Mary) remember my sister Annie saying that they usually spent one evening a week together, the Beachy youngsters walking to Lewis's one week and the Yoder's walking to Moses' the following week. They spent evenings visiting and singing and perhaps eating popcorn. A letter written by my father (Moses Beachy) tells that he sometimes went with the youngsters to sing at the Yoder's. Father loved singing and undoubtedly joined in with the singing at his home as well.

A letter from Eli describes one evening the Beachy and Yoder young people spent together when my brother Noah and sisters,

Annie, Effie and Amelia picked up Clarence, Eli, Amelia, Savilla and Amanda Yoder with the big sled and took them to Grantsville. Clarence stayed at John U. Yoder's with Albert till they came back. They considered going in to get Mandy at her home but saw a lantern going out to the barn and concluded that their barn work was not finished and so went on without her. Coming back to John's they went in there and visited for a while. Then Noah and Clarence went out to get the team of horses ready to go home. The rest were slow coming out and Noah sent Clarence in to inform them that he was starting home without them. He went a little way, then stopped to wait for them to catch up. They walked on past him and said they were going on a while. In a short while, as Eli describes it Noah came flying after them and looked so funny he just had to laugh at him. Seemingly, Noah (of all people), was cutting up that evening and drove into the side ditch in an attempt to upset the sled. Next, he asked Eli to drive, jumped out and tried unsuccessfully to push the sled over, so he got back on and seemed satisfied then. Eli states that they had more fun that evening than they ever had. Noah Beachy related that he and Eli went hunting together sometimes. One evening they caught a fox. So they stopped at John U. Yoder's and took it into the barn to show it to John. They then hid the fox and resumed their hunting but no more luck. Coming back to Johns they got the fox, took it back in and showed it to him again. John was quite impressed with their good luck at hunting foxes, two in one evening! Later when he learned what prank they had pulled on him he called Noah, "Der Shtuffer" (The Stuffer).

## Courting Years

As a young man, one of Eli's chief ambitions was to win the affection of Mandy Hershberger. Undoubtedly because of Mandy's attractiveness and Eli's shyness a young fellow with similar interests beat him to dating her. (This was when she was quite young for Eli was already dating her in 1913.) When Eli heard about the situation he made some remark about going with another girl if this other fellow has Mandy. But he never dated another girl. Quite likely he spent time in the secret closet about the matter and rejoiced when he learned that the couple had broken up. Eli did not lose too much time in going to the Sam Hershberger home to see if Amanda would accept his company. He said, "Ess ersht molh ess Ich gonga bin sie saena vord Ich nett sure ess Ich bliva darf so bin ich draus gablivva biss die andra ins bett gonga sin. Ovver noch selem bin Ich ny gonga." (The first time I

13

went to see her I wasn't sure if I would dare stay so I stayed out till the others went to bed. After that I went in when I got there.) Eli usually had a buggy rig to take Mandy home from the singing. Young folks gathered in a home, to which they were invited, on Sunday evenings and sang German songs in unison for an hour or more. Long buggy rides to and from singings were golden opportunities for visiting, and moonlight buggy rides held great potential for budding romances. According to Norman Bender, Eli turned his flash light on Mandy who was already in the buggy one evening and said, "Iss sie ovver nett shay?" (Isn't she pretty though?) On in between Sundays when there was no singing Eli often walked straight-cut across the Yost Yoder farm, then took another short-cut from Sim Lees' who lived along Niverton Road and through Lewis Yoder's sugar pasture to home.

Eli and his brother Clarence sometimes planned to beat each other home from seeing their girl friends. One night when he was walking Eli went straight to the barn to see if Clarence's horse was in the stable. It was, but he claimed the horse's tail was still swinging which told Eli that Clarence had just come home. A card written to Mandy indicates that Eli walked in all kinds of weather. He wrote that he had a bad cold because he got wet walking home through the rain on Sunday night.

Clarence, who went with a number of girls, advised Eli to try another girl instead of always going with Mandy. But Eli expressed himself thus; "Vell Ich hopp gore kay desire cott fer changa!" (Well I had no desire whatsoever to change.)

His brother Henry remembered Eli bragging how pretty, smart and quick Mandy was. He bragged about her dropping a knife and catching it before it hit the floor. When this was mentioned at their 50th wedding anniversary supper Eli said, "Sell vore davart bragga duvaya." (That was worth bragging about.)

While they were going with each other her mother had tuberculosis and Mandy was in charge of duties. This seemingly did not curtail their seeing each other. In 1916 when Barbara had whooping cough Eli's mother preferred that he should not go into the house for a time, probably to avoid carrying the whooping cough home to his little brother Norman. Possibly Eli had not had the cough himself. (Twenty years later Norman and Barbara became husband and wife.)

Eli's sister Mary, (Mrs. Eli Tice) remembers Eli having a pansy bed while he was at home yet. It is her opinion that he used to pick pansies from it to take along for Mandy.

Asked whether she used to visit in Eli's home while they were courting Mandy said, "Oh Ich vore alls a molh dott over net reglar. "(Oh I was there sometimes but not regularly.) This was an interesting observation of change of customs from the late Kate Hershberger's time to Mandy's time. Kate expressed shock to me about girls visiting in their boy friends' homes as they did in my young days. She would never have thought of visiting in her husband, Milt Hershberger's home while they were courting (in the 1890s).

## Rishta Fer Die Hochzeit
## (Preparing for the Wedding)

After four years of courting, Eli sent my father, Moses Beachy to Mandy as "Shteckli Monn." That is to interview her and be sure she was agreed to marry Eli before what heretofore had been kept strictly secret was publicly announced in a church service several weeks before the event was to take place. Eli said, "Ich vase nett yusht voss der shteckli monn gadu hutt. Ovver er hutts gadu all right!" (I don't know just what the "shetckli monn" did, but he did it all right!)

The week of the wedding Eli was at the bride's home to help get ready for the occasion. He really cleaned up the barnyard, picking up all stones and anything he could find to make it spic and span. Tuesday evening he and Mandy went to Grantsville. On the way home it started to snow huge fluffy flakes. It snowed all night and part of the next day, covering all of Eli's meticulous cleaning with a blanket of snow.

Eli's sister Savilla (Mrs. Jonas Tice) was also there to help prepare for the wedding. They put her to baking "Surprise cookies." Savilla was fearful that she would not do it right and repeatedly ask just how to go about it. After some of the cookies were baked Lizzie came around to check on them and remarked that they were nicer than hers were. Savilla really felt good about that. She got the recipe and often baked "Surprise" cookies.

On Wednesday evening Eli took the horses over to Hons Yoder's, where Joel Yoder's now live, to get their three-seated spring wagon (carriage) for the bridal party's use. The leaves were still on the trees and so loaded down with snow that he zigzagged in the road to avoid getting snow showered by hitting them as he went in the road from Milt Benders to Hons'.

15

# The Wedding

On Thursday morning October 25, 1917 the bridal party, Eli and Mandy, along with Clarence Yoder and Annie Schrock, Effie Hershberger and Elmer Schrock, their "nava hucker" (attendants) set out for the Flag Run Church in the spring wagon. Snow came up to the axle in some drifted areas and the horses stepped down through deep snow into mud.

Supposedly, the attendants kept in seclusion during the song service, which consisted of several German songs sung in unison, while Eli and Mandy met with the ministry in the anteroom for a period of instruction. During the last song the bridal party entered the church, arms coupled, with one couple in the lead and the other following the bride and groom to the front bench by the preacher's table (instead of a pulpit; had water to drink and books) where they were seated. After two sermons, scripture reading, and several prayers, Eli and Mandy joined hands to share the joys and sorrows of life, my father, Moses Beachy united them in marriage and pronounced them husband and wife. During the closing song the bridal party marched out to the anteroom, and the waiting spring wagon, leaving immediately for the bride's home.

The following "Thoughts of 50 Years ago" by Edna Miller, Maust depict the excitement Eli's wedding created at the Dutch College School.

*"As a school girl of 12 years, I well remember the excitement of the preparations for the first wedding of the three Hershberger families. At that time none of our Miller cousins or sisters or brothers were married. So of course our Hershberger school mates had a big start over us."*

*Then, when the wedding day came, those of us who could not stay out of school for the occasion, watched for the carriage (spring wagon) to come home from the wedding. Sure enough someone saw it coming around the corner down the road. And we did race to the outside. I guess the Yoder School porch was full. That was some experience for those of us from 10- to 15-years-old."*

On arrival at Mandy's home, dinner was prepared and served to relatives, ministers, and friends who were invited to the wedding dinner. Eli's sister, Savilla was a table waiter and her boy friend, Jonas Tice, was a "hostler" (a fellow who had the carriage waiting and also unhitched and took care of the horses). In the evening there was a singing for all the young people. They coupled up to go to the L-shaped table and after a period of singing German songs in unison, a full course supper was served to everyone present.

Mandy's sister, Barbara, who was three-years-old at the time remembers having been put on the high chair and given really good gravy bread to keep her occupied and out of the way while the busy cooks were getting dinner. At Norman Jr. and Leona Yoder's wedding reception someone inquired about the difference here and Eli's wedding and Mandy exclaimed that it was quite different, not much clean up now and she didn't know when they got through with all the stack of smeary dishes and things back then.

After the wedding Eli bumped a hanging lighted lantern in the cellar-way and threw it off the hook. But he threw his hands behind his back and caught it before it went crashing down the steps. (After fifty years of married life he commented that his wedding day was the happiest day of his life.) The following week Sam Hershberger's and Moses Beachy's took a trip to Canada to visit friends and Eli's did Sam's work. When they came back Eli's went on their honeymoon, traveling by buggy to Salisbury where they took the trolley to Meyersdale then a train to Washington, boarded a boat there and spent the night sailing to Norfolk, Va. The next morning they took a trolley out to the Amish settlement at Norfolk, were there over Thanksgiving and attended Mandy's school chum, Sadie Yoder and Simon Schrock's wedding. Homeward bound they went through Delaware, taking a boat from Cape Charles. The water was rough and Mandy got sick on this boat ride.

## Early Married Life

On their return Eli's stayed with her folks and Eli worked at different places until he was drafted. Noah M. Yoder then offered him a job on his farm which deferred him from going to camp. In March 1918 Eli's moved into the small house with Noah's who had four children (where Milt Yoder's lived until they built the new brick house, where Lewis Tice's now live.) Mandy helped with egg cleaning and packing for shipping by mail and Eli did the farming.

It was here that Eli lost a finger while grinding bones for the chickens. That spring Mandy and some of Noah's family including Noah had typhoid fever. She did not have the fever very hard but developed a cold and complications which caused her fever to rise to 105 one evening.

After the sick had recovered Eli and Noah built a tiny, two room

17

house with a cement floor to provide the privacy of a living and bedroom for Eli's. However they continued to cook and eat with Noah's family. In this little home they experienced joy when God blessed them with an apparently healthy baby boy whom they named Elmer.

Imagine their shock and sorrow when two days later while their helper was bathing him the baby developed breathing difficulty. Mandy, hearing him grunt said, "My ess mocht in ovver grexxa." (My but it makes him grunt though.) Very soon they realized that there was something drastically wrong with the baby and he passed away very unexpectedly of what the doctor diagnosed as acute heart failure. Although Mandy was not aware of doctors at that time suspecting her bout with typhoid fever early in her pregnancy as a contributing cause for the problem, today it would probably be considered as the cause.

## The Move to the Fisher Farm

In March of 1919 Eli's moved to what is now the Noah Fisher farm. On November 9, 1919 God again blessed them with a baby son, Henry. Anna Baker remembers being very much afraid that this baby would also die but he thrived on his parents' tender loving care.

That winter Eli's sow had more piggies than feeders. Mandy took three of the piggies into the house and fed them with a spoon until they were large enough to drink from a pan.

While living there Eli butchered and peddled meat. One day when he was grinding sausage he lost a second finger in the grinder. He quickly threw the belt off the grinder but when he opened the grinder his finger was lying in it. Mandy did not know how to harness a horse, so he managed to harness the horse and with her help hitch it to the buggy. Leaving Henry with Ethel Miller, the hired girl, they set off to Salisbury to the doctor. Eli's February 21, 1920 ledger lists a charge of $5.00, doctor bill, for dressing finger three times. On the way home they stopped at Ira Yoder's and asked Ira to come and finish the butchering job. Eli put his finger into a toothpick box, took it out and buried it.

## The Move to St. Paul, Pennsylvania

When Henry was a five-month-old thumbsucker Elis' moved down to St. Paul to what is now the Aaron Kinsinger farm. Here the Lord filled their quiver with six more children, Paul, 8-28-21, Ernest, 5-

18

16-23, Elizabeth, 10-30-24, Edna 9-1-26, Mabel 12-17-27, and Lena, 10-28-29. As was the custom at that time Mandy had a 10-day vacation in bed after the birth of each of her babies.

Mandy had none of the modern convenient gadgets such as teeter babes, strollers, infant seats or play pens to help in the care of her family. Small babies were tied onto the rocking chair or propped up with pillows to give them a change from lying flat. Creeping babies had freedom of the floor, exploring, getting underfoot and mopping the floor with their clothes. Boys as well as girls wore long, full-skirted dresses which needed to be pinned up out of the way to avoid hobbling the babies during the creeping stage.

Providing for a family of this size was not easy. Besides farming and raising rabbits and guinea pigs, Eli pursued many other projects to provide for his family. His 1926 diary reveals that he built a brooder house, made improvements in the barn such as cementing a feeding room and a manure pit, dug and hauled coal from a mine on the farm, butchered and delivered meats to stores, went out to farms to do butchering for neighbors and operated a sugar camp. In addition to this he picked cherries, planted and harvested cabbage, strawberries and raspberries and delivered these as well as butter and eggs to stores. Besides this he did some custom farming.

Records also show that he had the agency for Simplex brooder stoves and sold 24 during 1921. At this time his brother Menno was serving as hired hand for $30.00 a month and the two of them did take time out for hunting, both for sport and additional income.

His rabbit sales in 1926 totaled $633.47. Many were breeders and obviously some were special breeds; does selling for $3.00 to $10.00 and bucks from $1.50 to $4.50 each. They were shipped as far as Kalona, Iowa . Elmer and Andy Hershberger, sons of Jacob Hershberger of Norfolk, Virginia, bought a $7.00 doe and a buck for $1.50.

Eli's 1926 Diary indicates that my brother Noah Beachy and Eli continued their friendship and spent time together after their marriages. Mandy and Noah's wife Elizabeth Tice Beachy were first cousins as well as good friends. (From March 7th to May 27th the four of them were all the same age.) When Noah's Rachel was a baby Noah's were visiting at Eli's, Elizabeth wanted to go and help Mandy with the dishes. She took Rachel into the living room where she knew Noah had been sitting and although he did not eagerly reach for her she plunked the baby into a lap. Then she discovered that the men folks had exchanged places and she had put Rachel onto Eli's lap. (Many years later Noah's two sons married two of Eli's daughters.)

19

In his diary, for Wednesday, September 1, 1926 Eli wrote, "took care of the little girl, Edna." (The diary in it's entirety, along with other records and items of interest can be found in the appendix of the book.)

## The Beginning of Yoder Meat Packers

In 1927 at a cost of $76.44, Eli built a shed in which to do butchering, hardly dreaming that the project would develop into what is now known as Yoder Meat Packers. A unique feature of this shed was a folding smoke house. When not in use it was folded back against the walls, and presto Eli had a shed for his buggy. The shed housed an open-kettle furnace where water was heated. Hot water was carried to a barrel outside into which hogs were plunged to be scalded, then pulled onto a wooden platform where they were scraped and hung on a wooden tripod to be gutted and split. Hog halves for processing were carried into the shed on Eli's shoulder. While a gasoline engine operated the sausage grinder, the sausage stuffer, the lard press and saws were man-powered.

Eli opened a coal mine and did mining. He hired teams to haul a car load of coal to West Salisbury for shipment by rail. By the time the coal reached its destination business had become dull and the buyer was not satisfied with the quality of the coal. Payment for the coal did not cover the cost of hauling and shipment. This was quite a loss to Eli's.

They also operated a sugar camp on the Kinsinger farm. Eli had lost a lot of sleep with sugaring, a sick cow and a sick horse. One night he came in late and said, ("Vell Mommy, Ich bin froh ess Ichs so gute nemma conn ess Ich der syrup vidder ferbrenned hopp." (Well Mommy, I'm glad I can take it so well that I burned the syrup again.) He had fallen asleep on the job.

## Childrens' Activities

With their growing family Eli and Mandy now graduated to being "Pap and Mam," as the children called them when they were small. In later years they called them Dad and Mother (as they will be referred to from here on).

It was at the St. Paul farm that Dad patiently tried to teach Henry to say "drink" or "vasser" instead of "how", when he wanted a drink. He got him to repeat the words after him and thought his lesson had succeeded but immediately afterward Henry was thirsty and said "Boy how", "Boy", was what they called him at that time.

Here was where Paul's underside got warmed when he punched Henry with a sharpened pencil when he had crossed his will. Mother explained that the safest way to get the barn chores done was to put Ernest in the crib with his bottle, Paul in the living room and Henry in the kitchen each with play things, doors closed so they couldn't get together. Her chief concern was not so much to avoid scrapping but accidents, particularly that the baby carriage which tipped easily might get tipped and throw the baby out. Between milking cows she went to the house and peeped in the windows to be sure all was well.

Here was the pantry, (whose door was supposed to be closed) where Ernest had fair play while Anna Baker who was working there and Mother were outside. He had gotten into the lard and apple butter leaving not only a path from one crock to another but made a grand mixture of lard, flour and apple butter and decorated himself, his clothes and the pantry with it!

Seemingly, Ernest had a gift of getting into things and making cute remarks. One day Mother sent him to the pantry to get "sivva" (seven) crackers. He came out with both hands loaded and said "Ess vott net sivva. (It doesn't give seven.) He had been counting in English which has no sivva! One evening the children were eating cookies and one of the children consulted Mother on how many they could have. She set a limit and Ernest piped up and admitted that he had already eaten seven, which was well beyond the limit.

It was also here that the little boys played in the sand pile and paid no heed when Mother called them in for dinner, until they saw her coming to get them. Then they ran for the house. But Mother sometimes stopped them and applied a little switch she had broken from a tree on her way out. One day Henry, Paul, Ernest and Elizabeth made paint with a mixture of mud and water and were busily painting the shop walls a rich color when the dinner call came. There was no response to the call until they saw Mother coming. Quickly the children tried getting out another door and convincing Mother that they were coming. But this time she stopped them and used the whip. Elizabeth escaped, either because she was young enough to be excused or because she slipped through while Mother was busily occupied with the boys. Henry recalls the application as having been quite mild but it was effective in teaching the children obedience.

Undoubtedly Mother's gentle but firm manner of not sparing the rod and spoiling the child bore the fruit which Ruth Beiler observed years later when Mother got response to her requests without raising her voice. Elizabeth says her father seldom said much to correct her but he did give her a certain look sometimes which made her uneasy and she knew what it meant.

One day when Ernest was about four-years-old, Tillie Wengerd Beachy had just cleaned up the living room. When Ernest came in and saw everything so neat he dumped the block box and started to play. Tillie insisted that he pick his scattered blocks up again. Although inwardly rebelling he slowly picked them up murmuring "Ich vunner voss sie failed. Ich vunner voss sie. failed." (I wonder what ails her. I wonder what ails her.) Tillie says Ernest was her pet in the many years she worked for Dads and she had never demanded anything like that from him before that day.

One day the boys were playing with their new toy guns. Paul was the rabbit and had not only been shot, but eaten. When Mother asked him what that was lying on the floor if he was eaten he said, "Oh sell iss yusht der grutza, der grose grutza ess to layga iss." (Oh this is just the cob, the big cob that is lying here.) Paul was referring to what was left of the consumed rabbit like the cob of an ear of corn or the core of an apple.

On a day when Ernest had a cold Mother told him to blow his nose. Ernest said "Ich hopp geshter!" (I did yesterday.) When Dads' went to visit their neighbors, Gid Petersheim's, Mother instructed the children not to ask for candy. After a time of visiting in the living room Ernest went to the kitchen and walked around sniffing. Then he said "Ich schmock gore dictick candy."(I smell candy real, real much.) Obviously his nose was clear that day! Petersheim's took the hint and promptly brought the candy around.

One day Dad hitched the horses into the spring wagon and left Paul sitting on the spring wagon playing with the lines while he got guinea pigs ready for shipment. Evidently Paul pulled on the wrong line. Anyway the horses made a sharp turn and upset the wagon. When it stopped one of the posts was resting on Ernest's head. Little Paul tried so hard to lift it off but he couldn't budge it. Mother, who had been hanging up clothes came running to the rescue. After the excitement was all over she could not remember where she had left her clothes basket. The Lord graciously spared anyone from being seriously hurt.

On a day when Ernest had done something that required discipline Mother led him to the bedroom. He was crying and making a big fuss when suddenly the crying stopped and he burst out laughing. The children on the other side of the closed door wondered what had happened. They joined in laughing when they learned that Mother's rather flimsy switch had broken!

Mother kept her children busily occupied. The little boys stood on small benches and washed dishes until the water was cold and greasy.

When they were older the boys helped with hay making. Dad was in the hay mow, Mother "stuck the fork" and little Henry drove the team to pull the hay up. When Henry, who was small for his age, was older but still quite small he helped with hay making at the St. Paul farm. Going to the field with a team of horses and wagon, Dad then pitched large forks full of hay on the wagon from the rows raked up with a horse-drawn hay rake. The little fellow on the wagon really had to scramble to spread the hay out on the wagon and avoid getting covered with it. When the wagon was loaded, Dad got up on the load and drove the team in to the threshing floor of the barn. He then climbed up into the hay mow where his job was to spread the hay out evenly on the mow to make a nice stack. Mother left her work at the house and came out to help. Climbing on top of the load she spread out the arms of the huge three-pronged fork and plunged it down into the hay jumping on it to drive it in to make it take a big bite of hay. She then clamped the two arms together, now loaded with hay. Henry then drove the team of horses which were harnessed together with a double tree attached to the other end of the rope. By means of a system of pulley and a track and carriage the loaded hay fork rose straight up to the carriage then rolled over to the mow and when Dad told Mother to trip it, she pulled on a second rope which caused the fork to open and drop the hay. Quickly Dad spread it out and was ready for the next fork full Mother sent up. When all the hay was off the wagon Mother hurried back to her household duties while Dad and Henry went back to the field for another load. Henry also remembers harrowing when he was quite small and fearful of bears being in the woods by the field.

When Jonas Tice's visited at Dads' with their tribe of boys, all the boys had a jolly time running in circles through the living room, bedroom and kitchen. Occasionally they played in the barn and didn't want Elizabeth tagging along. So they made growling sounds from holes they had dug under the hay to frighten her. Their scheme did not work. Elizabeth paddled to the house and reported to the ladies what the boys were doing and went right back out again.

Edna's bottle was her chief consolation. When anything happened that upset her she ran to get her bottle. Dads' kept some goats that furnished the milk which Dad credited for making Lena chubby and rosy-cheeked. Being genuine goats they got into mischief such as climbing on top of a pickup load of egg cases as well as eating the registration card out of the pocket in Ed Yoder's touring car when they were Sunday dinner guests at Eli's. The boys had lots of fun rolling tires and watching the goats run after them.

23

When Henry and Paul started to school at St. Paul neither of them could speak English. Eventually their pictures were taken and when the photos were sent home with them they stopped along the way and tried to sell them to different people. Their neighbor, Mrs. Gideon Petersheim did not want any pictures and pointedly remarked that some people did not think it was right to have pictures. Needless to say Dads' were quite embarrassed when they heard of their sons' salesmanship. One day when the three oldest boys were taking a walk their neighbor's retarded son came down to the road and stood watching them with his hands crossed on his back. Then he said, "Dir sind all dry so shay vee pigs!" (All three of you are as nice as pigs.)

## Neighborly Deeds

While living at St. Paul, Dads' often did many kind deeds for their Hostetler neighbors. Johnny in particular often needed assistance with something he was unable to handle and he liked to be taken places. One day Mother was very eager to get out to work in the garden but it was a day when Johnny dropped in and was in his usual talkative mood. Mabel, just a little girl, was waiting to go out with her mother and becoming impatient. So she walked over to Johnny who was sitting on the coal box, took hold of his hand and said, "Cum, Chonny, doe ganea mir," (Come, Johnny, here we go).

While Tillie Wengerd Beachy was going to school from Dads and working for her board the Hostetler's needed assistance and Dads shared Tillie with them to help them out with milking etc.. Tillie was not too much enthused about the set up and thought Mother's cooking was better. She would stop in at Dads on her way home from school and raid their cupboard before going on to Hostetler's. She remembers how good the cold dumplings she found there tasted.

At the time of the 1927 split in the Amish church Dad and Mother stayed with what became known as the Beachy group under the leadership of Moses Beachy (now Mt. View Christian Fellowship). In time, automobiles were sanctioned in the Beachy group, and great was the excitement of the boys when they came home from school and saw a model T pickup truck in the barn yard. Dad had traded his faithful horse, Frank, "even up" on the truck. (This was the horse that Dads' brother Menno bragged about being so smart that he always went to Lewis Yoders' Menno's home after church without being guided. The horse got loose during service one Sunday and went over to Lewis' without Menno.)

Later Dad purchased a 1926 Dodge as a family car. What a thrill

24

for the children to go to church in a horseless carriage. One daughter recalls the grinding sound of the Dodge as they descended the hill from St. Paul down to the Kinsinger farm. Now that Dad had a car, Johnny Hostetler liked to go with him as well as to be taken places. Dad's records show frequent small fees for having taken Johnny somewhere. On one occasion when Johnny was paying for a longer ride than usual he reminded Dad, "Ich denk die cumpany vore auw eppes varte." (I guess my company was worth something too.)

On a Saturday evening when the temperature was dropping Dad thought of the deep ruts in the road going past the farm. He was quite concerned about it and said, "Now if it freezes tonight those ruts will be deep and rough and may damage people's cars." Although it was quite late he went out, hitched the team onto the drag and dragged the road, to smooth the ruts over.

## The Move to Maryland

In 1931 Dad sold the Kinsinger farm, had an auction sale and moved with his family to the Sam Hershberger farm, Mother's former home. Baby John was born December 23, 1931 to complete the family.

For the boys, moving from St. Paul to Yoder School involved a major adjustment. Mr. Francis Showalter, their teacher at St. Paul, kept order, the room so quiet that one could hear a pin drop. So strict was he that even well-behaved Henry got an undeserved but thorough "shaking-up" one day. At that time, when Yoder School was at its lowest ebb and had only one teacher, discipline was non-existent. The boys found whispering, giggling, much noise and students walking about at will, quite distracting. Then too lessons were too easy to be challenging. For example, at St. Paul they had 20 spelling words a day; then coming to Yoder school the assignment was 20 words for a week.

## Butchering Increases

The following year Dad built a 16' X 26' butcher shop at a cost of $368.35 with an additional $99.00 for equipment. The shop was quite an improvement over the shed in St. Paul, allowing him to do every-thing inside. It boasted a coal-fired boiler to heat water, render lard and operate a steam powered engine to run sausage and lard grinders. He now added custom butchering and canning of meat to his services and expanded deliveries to Grantsville and Frostburg, Maryland. During the first winter Dad had three custom jobs; the next year business had increased to 12 jobs!"

This was during the depression when everything was dull. Dad charged only one cent a pound for going out to farms, killing hogs and taking them to the shop for processing and delivering the processed meat to customers. Sausage dropped to a low of 16 cents a pound. Yet, in spite of all the odds against it, business thrived necessitating several additions to handle the trade which, due to lack of refrigeration, was limited to winter months.

Wages at that time ranged from 15 cents an hour for a beginning teenager (not a boarder); $3 to $4 a week for girls (except in rush seasons they received as much as $7 a week for several weeks) and $35 to $45 a month for men, including room and board.

During this time Mother, who was an excellent cook was cooking not only for her sizable family but for the butcher crew as well, which added up to 15 at the table for the noon and evening meals. Everyone enjoyed her delicious meals, especially the home-made bread. Since most of the food was raised and preserved right on the farm Mother needed a hired girl during the summer months to help with gardening and canning.

# Berries

A 1933 ledger records Dad having bought 2000 raspberry and 6225 strawberry plants that summer, providing plenty of planting and hoeing to keep his growing boys busy. The following summer the Lord blessed them with a tremendous yield of 16,000 quarts of strawberries, 3000 on one picking. Many berries were picked on shares, some sold locally and some shipped to Pittsburgh, Pa. Dad paid 2 cents a quart for picking and sold the berries at from 7 to 10 cents a quart. One day when the boys (and everyone else) were tired of picking berries they picked some that were too green. Dad said, several times "Nett vidder so du," (don't do that again) and that was all there was to it. Ruth Beachy Beiler, who worked there through the strawberry season, never heard Dad bawling any of the pickers out and he was always strictly honest in his sales. No one went away with a basket that was less than full. When he paid her he did not short-change but usually gave her a bonus. It was while Mary (I) was helping to pick berries and Henry checked her berries in that she first observed that he was a pretty nice chap.

# Helper's Recollections

Impressions that Ruth Beiler gleaned during her stay at Dads' were the quiet correction and obedience of the children. To her, Mother seemed the perfect mother because she did not neglect family worship but conducted it herself when Dad was absent.

Ruth remembers the delicious noon and evening meals that Mother had waiting for them when they came in hot and weary from working in the sun. She recalls Mother's tiny feet flitting to and fro as she prepared a meal on the hot coal stove and the huge, delicious loaves of bread she baked. Then there were the heaps of sewing and the stacks of mending to do on Mother's sewing machine. Yet she can not recall of ever hearing Mother speak of being tired.

Another recollection of Ruth's is the powerful voices of the little girls as they sang, playing church on the upper porch, and the sudden change of one voice into a woeful baby's cry. Quickly the "little mother" jumped up and dashed out of the "church" with her doll to quiet its sobs. Then there is the memory of Mother's strong voice as she sang about her work. Henry and Paul sometimes got the giggles at the table and Paul's eyes were so full of dancing mischief that Ruth had trouble controlling herself.

Mabel Hershberger Yoder (Mrs. Henry L.) who helped during butcher seasons also remembered some childrens' activities. One day when the little girls were playing visitors they all gave themselves names except Lena, who kept her own name. Then she cried because the others could be someone else and she just had to be herself. When Mabel came around with a partly eaten candy bar she saw that the children were noticing it and offered them a bite. One of the little girls eyed her and said "Ich vill nett dy schleck." (I don't want your lick.) When John was less than two-years-old Mabel picked him up and tossed him in the air and he slobbered right down into her mouth.

Mabel related how sad was the day when scarlet fever struck and as a result "Betsy" the little girl's much cherished rag doll had to be disposed of. There were no ministers to preach a funeral sermon but some real heart aches and possibly some tears from the would-be mothers. She remembered Lena's fashion of saying "Svill nett," (it doesn't want to) when she was asked to do something. On a Sunday morning when Mother told her to blow her nose real good before they leave for church Lena leaned against the kitchen wall and exclaimed, "Svill nett!"

Mabel Yoder Schrock, a daughter, recalls an incident when she flatly refused to wear the coat she was supposed to wear to go outside to play. Mother took her to the hall and spanked her to make her give up.

One year an extra nice lot of hogs got sick. The vet said, "Cholera! The best thing you can do is shoot them and get them out of here." So Dad shot $500.00 worth of hogs and the rendering company hauled them away. This was a major loss in depression times.

When John was a little fellow, he stood in front of the mirror one day and said, "Ich feel so shay, ovver vonn Ich in der shpeigle gook bin Ich nett." (I feel so pretty, but when I look in the mirror I'm not.) When Mother was explaining to the children the importance of being ready when Jesus comes, John thought a bit and said "Ich vill ersht shtroe nunner du." (I want to put straw down first.)

## Family Concerns and Hospitality

Obviously Dads' desired to have their growing family usefully occupied and provided that opportunity for them. During the summer they raised beans, tomatoes, cabbage and corn not only for themselves but for market. Then too the boys had their own projects of rabbits and guinea pigs to care for.

Dad's concern for their family was not only in keeping them occupied. They were deeply concerned about their spiritual growth as well and nurtured them faithfully with the practice of Bible reading and prayer. The provision of good literature and the encouragement to read it had immeasurable influence on the children. They have fond memories of their mother gathering them around her to teach them to sing. Her singing about her work also influenced the Yoder children to become a singing family.

Hospitality was a staunch practice. If someone happened to be at Dads' at meal time they were invited in to share Mother's delicious meals. Early morning cabbage loaders thoroughly enjoyed a hearty breakfast of hominy, pork pudding and apple sauce with the family.

One summer the Byrnes' family from Eckhart, Md., were invited out for a homemade strawberry ice cream supper. They appreciated it so much they spoke of it years later. In 1957 when Elizabeth and some of her daughters were in Byrnes' Store they spoke about the ice cream supper. And, true to their custom they immediately treated the girls to ice cream bars. Then one of the men handed Elizabeth one too saying that she looked more natural with that in her mouth. Her good intentions of walking past the candy real fast so she would not be tempted to buy any was defeated for they not only gave them candy but sent some along home for the rest of the family.

28

The girls were very fond of babies. It was a coveted privilege to be first to tell of the arrival of a new baby in the community. When there was baby news they raced home from school to be the first to tell it. On one occasion Edna enthusiastically related what a wonderful time they had because they had had enough company with enough babies to reach around so that they didn't have to take turns holding them. Irvin Beachy's Phoebe and Carol were almost adopted as nieces and when their twins came along Dad's girls were just as thrilled as their real aunts were. After all, Tillie having worked so many years for Dads' seemed like a member of the family.

Elizabeth's love for babies initiated her dream of a whole house full of children plus a baby in a blanket. She was concerned lest the family register for eight children in her new Bible would not be have enough space for all her children. (She fell two short of filling that, but her 26 grandchildren have more than filled the space provided for them long ago!)

As a young girl Elizabeth had a habit of saying, "Ich vutt sverr shunt gadue. Es nemmt so long." (I wish it were already done. It takes so long.) Her siblings teased her about never getting a husband because she thought it takes too long and wished it was done already. But she beat them all to the marriage altar!

As non-resistant Christians, Eli's sons registered as conscientious objectors when drafting came up during World War II. Henry, Paul, and Ernest were in the age bracket making them eligible for alternate service. However, during C.P.S. days Dad rented several farms and really pushed farming at the time. The local draft board stated that they could not put them anywhere that they would be more useful than they were right where they were. Henry concluded that even though he was not drafted as other young men in the area were, his life plans were postponed just the same as those of men who were drafted and he buckled down to doing his best right where he was.

Dad and his sons raised acres and acres of peas, corn and beans for the local cannery which Dad had been very influential in getting into the area. His interest here was not so much for his own benefit as for the economy of the community.

He, along with others, had invested quite a bit of money in this venture. Unfortunately, the company folded up and those who had invested in it lost their money. The "Pea Viner" buildings were adapted for what is now the Grantsville Auction on Route 669 and the "Cannery" down by the Casselman River housed the Casselwood Furniture factory until recently it was sold.

Meanwhile, Mother was not only busy caring for her family's

needs but conscientiously teaching her maturing daughters both basic domestic duties and detailed economic pointers such as avoiding thick vegetable and fruit peelings, scraping kettles and bowls clean, never to leave a knife lying upright where someone might reach into it or in a pan of trimmings where it could get into garbage and find its way to a pig's stomach. She had them take weekly turns working in the butcher shop or in the house. Along with household duties they also learned the art of milking, separating and churning butter, plus all the many experiences needed for capable housekeeping.

Elizabeth became aware of special dishes, like puddings, cakes etc. appearing on the table that the girls did not know were around. They concluded that their mother was preparing these treats after the family was in bed.

During the 1941 butcher season when Mother was getting dinner, a skillet handle overturned and poured hot lard into her shoe, causing third degree burns and huge blisters. The girls really had to hustle to get things done when Mother was not able to help. Rhoda Schrock Yoder helped out for a while, but Mother was soon getting around by kneeling the sore leg on a chair and helping as much as she could.

# Reaching Out

About 1944-45, Dad bought the Dr. N.R. Davis farm and rented it to his sister Mary, the Eli Tice family. The underlying purpose of this was to give them a home and occupation for their growing family in the home community. (Elis' had been living on the Black farm near Garrett, Pa., in an undesirable environment for the children.)

One hot summer day when Menno Hershberger's men folks were helping on the farm, Mother prepared a platter of sausage for dinner. After the men had gone back to the field she discovered the sausage in the warming closet. She was really "Aus gabutta!" (Beat out). Feeling badly about it and thinking that the men were working hard and really needed meat she made sausage sandwiches in the afternoon and sent them out to the field for them.

In 1943 the barn was remodeled, a milk house built and milkers installed in preparation to sell Grade A milk, thus eliminating milking by hand, separating and churning, from the ladies' many duties.

During the 40s Mother sometimes shared her girls as hired help during the summer months. Elizabeth and Edna each spent a summer working for their Uncle Norman and Aunt Barbara and Mabel was there two weeks when Catherine (Mrs. James Beachy), was born.

Dad also let his sons help out on various projects. When Henry was helping with the building of the new Maple Glen Church he fell off a scaffold, but was not seriously hurt. In 1944 he fell from the top of the silo chute and again the Lord spared him from serious injury. This time he needed to use crutches for a while but his leg healed up nicely.

By this time dating had become popular among the Yoder youth. Within 12 years after Elizabeth's marriage to Ernest Beachy, October 21, 1945 they were all married, Henry to Mary Beachy, 5-25-47, Paul to Marie Miller, 7-5-53, Ernest to Lena Yoder, 4-22-51, Edna to Claude Beachy 1-1-49, Mabel to Raymond Schrock, 5-1-49, Lena to Elmer Beachy, 8-29-52, John to Grace Yoder, 4-18-57.

In 1946 Mother had major surgery. When she left the house to go to the hospital she remarked, "What God does is done right." Undoubtedly her faith in God's best way contributed to her rapid recovery.

# The Locker Plant in 1947

Over the years increasing business had necessitated several additions to the butcher shop and Dad's vision of serving the community better was shoving the shop's walls again. Consequently, early in 1947 when Henry informed his father of his engagement to Mary Beachy and his plans to be doing something for himself, Dad offered to build a locker plant if Henry was interested in operating it. Construction of the Locker Plant began in May of 1947 and Dad's dream of a Locker Plant to serve the community became a reality when its doors opened in December of 1947. Dad then formed a business partnership with his sons, Henry and Paul, Henry and Mary moved into the east end twin apartment above the Locker and Henry operated the Locker Plant.

During the winter of 1948 Mother was seriously ill. They carried her out and put her into the Nash (family car) to take her to the hospital. It was cold and stormy and the Nash refused to run. They hitched a tractor to it and pulled it over to Menno Hershberger's (now Simon Tice's) and transferred her to Menno's car to take her to the hospital. Her blood count was so dangerously low that Dr. Solosko later admitted that he was fearful she would not respond to transfusions.

After five blood transfusions and minor surgery the Lord restored mother to good health. Melvin Beiler was one of the blood donors... Several days later when he came to the hospital to see his wife and baby daughter, Judy Mae, Dad was there visiting Mother. He clasped Melvin's hand with a hearty thanks pressing a ten dollar bill into his hand. Melvin did not expect this but Dad insisted. By this time Mother was a lot better and Dad joked a bit, saying, "Ich vase nett vie des shoffa scaled vonn Ich die Mandy hame nemm mit all dem mon's bloot in sich" (I don't know how this is going to work when I take Mandy home with all these men's blood in her).

The Locker Plant had done nothing to alleviate the crowded condition of the butcher shop. In 1949 Dad's dream of a new butcher shop to produce quality meats and provide jobs for local people also became a reality. When the slaughtering was moved to the new shop which was built onto the locker Mother discontinued cooking for the butcher crew.

By 1952 the demands of the locker plant and his growing sons' need for outdoor freedom resulted in Henrys' moving to their new home. Since then various families and finally several maiden ladies have occupied the apartments above the locker plant and the one above the butcher shop was renovated to serve as additional offices and the ladies' lobby.

Over the years Claude and Olive Yoder and Dad and Mother had many enjoyable times together, traveling together to the New England States, Canada, and Florida as well as on other excursions. Soon after they started making bologna at the Locker an unidentified caller phoned Dad and asked him for the bologna recipe. Dad emphatically informed the man that they had paid for the recipe and were not handing it out. Smothering laughter and in a disguised voice the man sounded very disappointed, and continued to beat about the bush whether there was not some way he could get the recipe. Dad was firm. No way would he let this man have the recipe! Finally the caller asked whether he could buy some bologna if he came to the shop. Dad assured him that he could, and at last asked who was calling. "Well, they'a, they'a used to'a to call me Sport," was the reply. Then such laughter. It was Claude Yoder pulling a prank. Claude was also known as "Sphundly" and gave Olive the name "Pansy" because, said he, she was as pretty as a pansy while Dad called Mother his morning glory because she was always as bright and cheery as a morning glory. (This was back in the days of party lines and I (Mary) was on the upstairs phone laughing along with Claude because I had recognized him at once.)

## The Farm Is Sold

In 1955 Dad and Mother sold the farm to their daughter Mabel and her husband, Raymond Schrock, and temporarily moved into the apartment above the butcher shop until their new home across the road from the Locker was completed. Retirement from the farm did not mean idleness. Dad continued to kill and cut up hogs, deliver meat, and attend cattle sales, while Mother did the laundry and some cleaning around the Locker. She served two years as president and two years as vice president of the Mt. View Sewing Circle. At the time of Grandma Yoder's (Mrs. Lewis Yoder) death the Mt. view Sewing had over 100 of her pieced quilt tops on hand. Mother prepared lining and backs for these as well as other pieced quilt tops for the sewing.

Mother was always one of the first to be on the job when there was any relief canning or freezing to be done. And she stuck to the job until the clean-up and everything was finished.

# A Near Tragedy

In January of 1959 a major tragedy was barely averted when carbon monoxide gas spread through Dads' house because of a blocked chimney. His report verbatim of the episode in the Lewis Yoder family letter follows:

*"But we want to be satisfied however the Lord wants it to be and feel very thankful to Him for all His blessings and his protection over us during the monoxide scare we went through. Also to all the folks that helped us through so good. Monoxide Gas is odorless and tasteless and you can't see it. It's just there and you don't know it. And if you are in with it you get dumb-headed and can't think right. When Lizzie Tice went to the basement to wash Monday morning she got sick all at once. She could think enough to come up in the house and crawled up the steps so she don't fall. That morning I was in the basement before going to the plant. When I came over to the plant to kill hogs I felt it going around in my head a little. Mandy went to the basement to see if she can smell any gas. She said "No gas there." Well, Mother called Jonas, and they fetched Lizzie. Monday P.M. I went to the sale, Mandy feeling better. Tuesday morning she felt extra good, so she washed dishes and I went to work and she was to come to doctor about 11 o'clock. I told her I'll be over about that time. So 15 till 11 she got up to get ready to go to doctor, then answered the telephone yet, but felt real bad so she lay down again. I came over just that time. She said she can hardly go to the doctor. So I said she shall rest and I'll go out and talk to him. (Grantsville) and came back in a few minutes and found her unconscious on bed. Called Paul over from plant. (Henry already gone home.)*

*So Paul called doctor tried the third one. So Dr. Rock came from Meyersdale. All this time I was standing in front of the bed fanning Mandy as that was all I could think of to do for her besides praying. Paul was busy on the telephone, called doctor again in about 20 minutes to be sure he was coming. About that time he came in. Before Dr. came I felt once that I feel real bad. Dr. went behind the bed I in front. I remember he started to examine her and that was the last I can remember, but was still standing in front of the bed. Dr. thought Mandy has a stroke and explained things and asked what my desire is, to treat her at home or have her taken to the hospital. I of course didn't know or hear anything he said. So, soon they saw I was going down. So Paul and doctor took me to the davenport and laid me down. So of course doctor thought this was a shock for me that I passed out. Henry came and by that time Paul passed out. Doctor of course thought this is also a shock on Paul to have Mom and Dad both down. Very soon doctor felt something too, but never before had a shock worked on him like that. (That's what he said.) Dr. was getting sick and left us three half-dead lay. He thought Paul and I will be alright soon then we can decide what to do with Mother, bring to the hospital or treat at home. Dr. was affected he couldn't think right anymore. So he left for Mey. took him 1 and 1/2 hour to go home. Over at Cross Roads he pulled off the road and passed out but finally started out again but he don't know how he got home. Then Mrs. Rock helped him into the house and got a doctor for him. They finally got Mandy to the hospital and the second doctor called up to bring me in too. Paul came to and they took him home. So they took me to the hospital and were both in one room and woke up about the same time. Henry was there and talked to me and said I'm better, Mom is too. So I turned my head and seen her in another bed. She looked at me and each cracked a smile at each other. I wondered how they got the hospital beds in our bedroom and what the nurses are doing here. Next I found out we were in the hospital. I felt something at my nose. A tube in the nose giving us oxygen. I said it's the first time I was ringed. They called our plumber in to examine the boiler. He said no gas in here. When he came home he felt it and called the Gas Co. in Frostburg. They came out and pulled out the stove furnace pipe and found plaster from the chimney fell down in and shut off draft left fumes (monoxide gas) in basement. Monoxide gas also comes from coal burners, car and tractor exhaust."*

In a later letter Dad referred to this experience having been the Lord's will and having brought him a wonderful blessing. Still another letter states about him having had doubts that all his sins were forgiven until when he woke up in the hospital it was revealed to him that "they were all covered." (Supposedly this was the time).

It could be added here that Mother was just recovering from a severe case of bursitis in her shoulder. To Dr. Rock who did not know about her having had bursitis her weakened arm was a symptom of a stroke. I (Mary) don't know what Dad referred to about a second doctor having called. Doctor Rock had collapsed when he came home and the doctor who came to check on him concluded that he had over done himself and gave him a shot that knocked him out for several hours. When he woke up he got on the phone to have a everyone gotten out of the house and call the gas company. This had already been done by that time. I (Mary) saw the doctor passing here on his way home and thought he looked terrible. I wondered what awful thing had happened at Dads to make him look so down and out.

Of the chinchillas housed in the basement only two survived, but Bobby, the canary, who was close by the dining room window was unharmed and singing cheerily the following day.

Dads were discharged from the hospital the following day. He was able to get dressed himself but she needed assistance. He was soon on the go again but Mother, whose exposure was longer, had a more lengthy recuperation. Now that Dad had more time he took up several hobbies. Since the fate of the chinchillas he had stopped raising chinchillas and set up a shop in the basement to build purple martin bird houses. This hobby mushroomed into a small business. He completely lost track of how many houses he built. They were sold locally and out of state. It is not unusual to see some of his once beautiful, now quite weathered martin houses as you drive through the countryside.

# Dad Was A Lover of Nature

Dad was a nature lover. The four martin houses and the large aquarium of colorful gold fish on their front lawn were evidence of his desire to share the beauties of nature with others and were a great attraction to customers who drove in at the locker. He was as tickled as a small boy with a new toy when a colony of martins accepted the first house he put up. So intent was he on favoring martins that even a bluebird that considered moving in was disposed of, and he kept adding houses to fill the needs of the birds. The houses were mounted on poles and can be laid down for cleaning. Each fall Dad cleaned them and closed the holes with plastic strips to keep the sparrows out. These were removed before the first scouts arrived in the spring. He loved his martins and spent hours sitting on the porch watching them. Coming home from the hospital after a bout with pneumonia, he paused on the lawn to talk to the martins before going into the house. It seemed the birds recognized him and were listening to him. Mother took care of goldfish customers. Occasionally the aquarium had to be restocked before the summer was over. Once the glass on one side of the aquarium fell out and dumped the fish onto the lawn. Fortunately it was discovered soon enough to save them. Twice an overly eager child fell into the aquarium.

Early in the sixties Dad built a rabbit and guinea pig house with an automatic watering, convenient feeding arrangement, and a garage attached. When guinea pigs proved to be more profitable, he filled the house with pigs and raised thousands of them. For many years he gathered up the animals of other growers and took them, with his to Scottdale, Pa.

One night a rat got into the guinea pig house and killed twenty young pigs. Dad was appalled and told his grandson, Moses, that he planned to stay up that night and shoot the critter. "Ya shees sie in svay,"(Yes, shoot it in two) advised Moses. "Ya, und noe noch a molh!" (Yes and then again!) exclaimed Dad. His plan to shoot the rat was unsuccessful but he managed to pen it into the wall where he poisoned it. In 1981 when he went out of the guinea pig business due to failing health, his carefully kept records showed that he had cleared $16,000 on the project.

## Mother's Cookies and Other Activities

Mother was also busy baking delicious ginger cookies and brown sugar cookies for the grocery store which was one of the many additions built on to the original locker buildings. Her cookies were much in demand and she sometimes stirred 25 pounds of flour into cookie dough in one day. By 1967 records showed that she had sold 125,208 cookies from 1959 to 1967. Besides these she nearly always had special chocolate cookies with frosting on hand for guests, which the grandchildren (and their parents) loved. She really enjoyed baking, singing as she worked and offering delicious, fat, hot cookies to anyone who came in. She continued baking until she was hospitalized in 1976 and had two batches of dough in the refrigerator waiting to be baked then. She always refrigerated her dough for several weeks before baking it so that she could handle it with less flour. Results: a super-soft delicious cookie! Her daughter Lena baked those two last batches of dough.

Mother spent many hours babysitting for grandchildren as well as stepping into the children's homes to help out in times of need. When Paul and his family had mumps Dad readily consented to Mother's going to the rescue and staying until they were all right again, but he informed Paul that when they don't need her anymore he wants her back! Then too Mother, not wanting anything to go to waste, regularly salvaged the contents of the grab box. (A box where unsaleable produce in the store was collected.) Apples ready to serve in apple sauce or stewed apples found their way to Paul's. Over ripe bananas were transformed into delicious banana bread and shared with the Locker partners. Even pick-out oranges were turned into delicious jam and shared with the partners.

Pondering over the success of Dad's ventures and his capable business management one would hardly suspect that he had only a fourth grade education. Yet, in speaking of school he always referred to how hard school work was for him and rather regretfully stated that he never did get farther than fourth grade. Nevertheless his 1911 report card when Savilla Bender was his teacher indicates that he applied himself diligently, his lowest grade having been 70 while most of them were in the 90's, and his deportment 95 and 98% for the parts of three months he attended school that term.

Back then school attendance was not compulsory. When there was farm work to do boys were kept at home to work. Undoubtedly irregular attendance was the reason for Dad's school difficulties. Anyway, his penmanship and figures would have put many a highly educated executive to shame.

# Kindly Deeds

Over the years Dad's home was not only an attraction to customers but an open haven of hospitality. Occasionally they had boarders who worked at the Locker. They took in three school-age grandchildren while their mother stayed in Baltimore with their hospitalized brother. Then too, they converted their home into a mini-nursing home to care for Mother's brother John who had suffered a severe stroke, took in Mother's sister Anna and her ailing husband, Calvin Baker, and again later when she was a widow. Furthermore Mother's sister Effie had her home with them for ten years.

Besides these kind deeds they provided transportation for folks who needed it, taking Mrs. Elmer Schrock along to church regularly. I (Mary) know of only one occasion when they forgot a passenger at the church house! The only time I am aware of that Mother's

37

hospitality may have appeared doubtful was when the late Jacob Hershberger was there for a meal and Dad told her to pass the cake to him. She said,"Err hutt cott." (He did have cake.) Then thoroughly embarrassed she quickly passed it to him! Dad teased her about that for a long time.

Mother did not like to see anything go to waste. When she had a surplus of something she found someone who could use it and if necessary canned or froze it for them. She canned for her mother-in-law after she was no longer able to do it herself, as well as for her children and a nephew of Eli's whose wife was not well.

## 50 Years of Married Life

In October 1967 the children celebrated their parents' fiftieth wedding anniversary with a family supper at the Casselman Restaurant Friday evening and open house in their home on Sunday afternoon. Although they would have been quite content to have no "fuss" made for their anniversary they did consent to the celebration. Mother however, with sincere modesty requested that no photos of them should be published in newspapers.

Much of the information herein was gleaned for "This Is Your Life" which was compiled and read as a surprise for them at the anniversary supper. Not knowing anything of the writing project they both cooperated beautifully in giving information. Consequently gleaning the material was lots of fun.

After fifty years of marriage their age and some arthritis was beginning to slow Dads down. Dad dropped hog killing and Mother relinquished the plant laundry to a younger lady, but they were still quite active.

The family will always cherish the memory of Mother's scrumptious Sunday dinners. Her fried potatoes were the best ever! Then there was the corn, sausage, carrot salad, grapenut or butterscotch pudding, pickles, cake or cookies and fruit or pie to top it off! Yum, yum!

In early years there were the Christmas gatherings in the farm house with gifts for everyone. Eventually choosing gifts for the increasing number of grandchildren became too much for Dads and each family received an envelope with an overwhelmingly generous gift. One year each grandchild received a silver dollar from Dad's collection. After the family outgrew Dad's house, family gatherings were held elsewhere but always Mother's special, much loved chocolate cookies with frosting, were available.

Choosing a useful and needed gift for Dads was difficult. While visiting at Henrys, Mother observed their secretary desk with a bookcase on top, inquired where they got it, and said it was just what they need. Her expression served as an inspiration. The family got together and bought a used secretary for them. Dad's birthday was coming up and as a scheme to get them away they were asked to bring guinea pigs over to Ernest Beachys' for Philip who had Dad's birthday and had rheumatic fever at the time. While they were away the family got together and placed the secretary in the house then we waited for them to come home. Ernest's also came as soon as Dads' left there.

Dads were quite surprised to see everyone there when they arrived home. Mother took a chair and set it right in front of the desk but didn't notice it, nor did Dad. There she sat and chatted. The granddaughters got the giggles and Mother was trying to discover what the fun was. Finally she went to the kitchen and seeing the dough tray, which had been moved to make room for the desk, standing there she looked around to see why it was out of its place. Then surprise! Her mouth dropped open and she was almost speechless for a bit. They really did make use of that desk.

Knowing that it would become quite late the family had decided that we could get together this one time without eating. After a while Dad got up and with a chuckle said, "Vell von dir nett icecream greega scalet vy doon Ich!" (Well if you aren't going to get ice cream I will!) He went over to the store, brought ice cream and potato chips and of course we wound up eating after all.

## More Expansion in the Business

As time went on, inspection laws and regulations became more and more demanding. A major expense that would never bring monetary returns was a $36,000.00 sewage plant. By 1970 federal inspection was a requirement for selling meat out of state, resulting in the need to refinance, enlarge and renovate the kill floor and coolers to meet the rigid inspection requirements. Along with this the present store and bakery were also added.

## Health Problems

At the age of 75-years Dad had gall bladder surgery. Mother, who was not aware of the many tubes needed for post surgery patients, was quite shocked when she went into the recovery room to see Dad. However he was blessed with a rapid and complete recovery.

39

In the spring of 1976 Mother was not feeling well for some time. Her blood pressure was alarmingly high and not responding to medication. On the afternoon of April 27th she was sewing on the machine. When she got up to do something else her leg did not function properly. They went to the doctor that evening and he sent them on to the hospital. By the next day, when Dad went in to see her she was not able to speak to him and her right hand was becoming helpless. This was quite discouraging for Dad. That evening when Henrys went down to the hospital with him again she had brightened up and was able to talk. I (Mary) had the privilege of combing and braiding her hair which she seemed to appreciate very very much.

That night she became confused and tried to get out of bed so from then on someone stayed with her round the clock. For several days her condition worsened and her speech was gone. One morning when Dr. Nafziger checked her he shook his head and said, "Well, the left side is having problems too." The next morning he called me (Mary) out to the hall and said, "Amanda had what we call a full blown stroke. She will always be a helpless invalid, never walk again or have the use of her right hand." He then advised making plans and preparations to care for a helpless invalid and take her home to her familiar surroundings in a few days.

For several weeks following her stroke Mother's hearing had improved unbelievably. She was able to understand normal talking without either of her hearing aids. After several weeks her hearing began to fail and she needed her aids again. Her hearing loss became worse over the years so that it was difficult to make her understand in the last years.

I (Mary) discovered one day that although Mother was not talking she was able to read and sing as well as repeat words, after you, when prompted to do so. Then one morning Joyce Beachy Maust entered her room and said "Good morning, Mandy," and to her surprise she responded with, "Good morning Mandy."

When Dad came in to see her that afternoon I prompted Mother to say "Hello" to him. His face lit up with surprise and his eyes filled with tears of joy at her greeting.

Physical therapy was started the last few days at the hospital, with Mabel and Mary observing so that they could give Mother some exercises when she went home. Meanwhile, Norman Yoder's hospital bed was set up at home in readiness for Mother's homecoming. She went home by ambulance slightly more than two weeks after being admitted to the hospital.

While Mother seemed glad to be at home, for a woman who had

always been so active serving others, to suddenly be helpless and on the receiving end was a terrifying experience and a major adjustment.

Exercises and therapy were not a pleasure for Mother. There were times when she was discouraged and would have preferred being left in peace. Sometimes it seemed to be painful and to wear her out. Nevertheless, with Dad's splendid coaching she always consented and cooperated with exercising. Quite often the Lord graciously let her drop off to sleep through a part of the ordeal. Then there was the question, is it being effective when there is no resistance? Apparently it was for her hand did not shrivel or close up and her grip became stronger. She faithfully squeezed the foam rubber ball we created for her and cooperated beautifully with trying to do things she was asked to try.

Joanna Yoder Schrock was aware that some folks at Goodwill Mennonite Home who could not speak were able to sing so we tried it with Mother and she sang right along (with words I was not sure of) as we sang "Gott Iss Die Liebe."

Then one morning when I was bathing her, she lifted her arm. And with a bit of encouragement reached it out to shake my hand. It was hard to tell who was the more delighted, I stooped and gave her a resounding kiss and we sang "Praise God from Whom All Blessings flow." When Dad came in from feeding his guinea pigs I prompted her to reach out and shake his hand. Again his face lit up and his eyes spilled over with tears of joy as he chuckled and eagerly clasped that hand. Undoubtedly his hearty chuckle at every new accomplishment in the weeks to follow did much to cheer Mother on and keep trying.

Then Mother gave us a scare. Dad phoned Henry's early in the morning to tell them she had been perfectly quiet all night long and he could not arouse her. Henry's left immediately. (Leaving their house looking as though the Midianites had fled.) Mother's pulse was very rapid and irregular nor did she respond to any attempts to rouse her. Dr. Nafziger advised having a nurse come in to check on her. Louise Maust who came, proceeded to examine her with no response. Then she flashed a bright light into her eyes and Mother woke with a start. She seemed bewildered to see us standing by her bed. The rest of the day she was very groggy, listless and somewhat confused. In a few days though, she seemed to be back to where she had been before this episode.

Later Dad met Katherine Miller, an LPN noted for rehabilitating stroke victims. "Yes," Katherine was interested in a job and would be available. She stepped in to take care of Mother during the day. Katherine was trained and capable of doing all those things which

Mabel and I were afraid to tackle without training. She soon had Mother out on the floor and in time she was able to take steps. Then too she got her dressed, removed the hospital bed and reinstated their own bed so that Dads could sleep together again, making things as nearly normal for her patient as was possible. Mother responded whole heartedly to these changes.

Dr. Nafziger had not recognized Mother's unfailing perseverance and determination. In time, these, coupled with many prayers, God's healing power, Katherine's coaching, and the encouragement of family and friends helped her to regain first her speech then limited use of her arm and finally walking.

With loving perseverance Katherine taught Mother to walk again, not with her former light, swift and springy step but "Always the right foot first!" For some time she walked unaided but after several falls, one on the porch where she scraped her forehead down over the brick wall, she was encouraged to use a walker. The "click click" of the walker became a familiar sound as she took countless walks through the house.

As her hand improved she took up pot-holder weaving and in 1976 gave each of the 46 grandchildren one for Christmas. Later she knitted yards and yards of leper bandages. (Her sister-in-law, Eli Mary, started and finished the bandages for her as her hand did not cooperate well enough to handle the more difficult steps of knitting.) Besides this she was able to help with the preparation of foods for canning and freezing and really became involved and excited about these projects. At times she did not think she needed to rest when there was something like that to be done, and would rest real fast! There was great rejoicing because her mind was clear and she was cheerful, often laughing instead of crying as many stroke victims do.

However things were not as they used to be, which sometimes became quite frustrating. For, instance she might say just opposite of what she meant to say when answering yes and no questions. This was frustrating to a young girl who helped care for Mother a short while and did not understand the cause of it. So, she concluded that Mother was either being picky or forever changing her mind. Then there was the hand that would not let go automatically. One day she looked at me (Mary) and very earnestly inquired "Fa voss vore nix so dafore?" (Why, was there nothing like that before?) On further questioning her she wanted to know "Vy a hont ess nett gay lust!" (Why, a hand that doesn't let go.) This was somewhat of a problem when shaking hands. Quite often she held on to a hand until she was asked if she could let go. One day after church Simon Beachy shook hands with her just as we were going out the door and she held on tight pulling his hand along. When I asked whether she can let go of his hand she dropped it immediately and as usual, was highly embarrassed.

Another real blessing was the fact that she could read. Sewing and writing were out. With her good sense of humor she was able to laugh at her "funny looking stitches" when she had tried to mend something of Dad's as well as at her weavy writing. Although writing was very tiresome for her she sometimes wrote a few lines for Claudes' or in the family letter. She spent many hours reading. Mother, in her favorite rocking chair reading her beloved Bible, was a treasured sight.

For several years Mother was able to get up from her chair and walk about in the house as she pleased. She walked often to avoid getting stiff. The longer she sat still the harder it was to get started again. Sometimes she would have difficulty getting her right foot to move and would say "Es seemed es vonn err fesht gaboppt vare." (It seems as though it was stuck fast.) After Katherine Miller went into VS up North, Rosanna Yoder, family members including nieces, and Tillie Wengerd Beachy took turns helping along.

During this time Mother's observations and her memory of where things were was amazing. One Sunday she noticed me (Mary) looking for something and asked what I was looking for. I told her" a pickle dish." She said "If they are where they used to be they're on the top shelf in the left hand corner." Also amazingly they were right there in spite of 5 or 6 years of different people having worked in her kitchen. Often though, when asked where to find something she would say, "Siss in die shuplaut" ("it's in the drawer"), leaving one to guess which of the 15 drawers in the kitchen or six in the dining room the wanted item was in.

Much as Dad enjoyed fishing he gave up that hobby and sold his boat to stay close by Mother. He did the gardening with her supervising from her rocking chair. She became quite worked up about getting things out in time and directed him in getting the seeds ordered early.

Always there were orders for martin houses and Dad was kept busy filling these. Mother was no longer able to help him with painting and he missed this. Now, as she went walking she often stopped by the basement door to call a cheery, "Hi, Mr. Yoder!" down to him. And he sometimes came to the foot of the stairs to return the greeting and give her a loving smile. Dad did continue attending auctions and delivering guinea pigs to Scottdale.

Besides all these duties he tenderly cared for his wife and often joined in to help with canning and freezing projects. They retained their sense of humor and sometimes got laughing spells, Dad with his hearty contagious laugh and Mother with a subdued chuckle, holding her hand over her mouth. On a day when Joanna Yoder Schrock was there they were preparing plastic strips for closing the martin house holes and Dad told Mother a piece was too short. Mother said, "Well, maybe you can cut a piece on." Then they laughed and laughed and laughed some more.

One Sunday morning when I was getting Mother ready for church I goofed and slipped her cape and apron on her before she had her dress on. That started her off in gales of laughter so that Dad came to the bedroom to see whatever was going on. She was laughing so that she could not tell him. He too went into stitches when I explained what had happened.

Dad was not hesitant to tell a joke on himself or laugh at his own blunders and joined in laughter at a freak accident of his. He was dreaming that a little dog was snapping at his legs and wanted to give the dog a good kick. "Wham," he hit the wall behind the bed! Fortunately, he didn't kick Mother but unfortunately he hurt his toe. Arthritis set in and it bothered him the rest of his life. Dr. Martin sat down on his haunches to examine the toe and when Dad told him what had happened he laughed so that he tipped over backwards and landed on the floor! Now it was Dad's turn to laugh!

Perhaps for Dad the hardest thing to give up was regular church attendance. How he rejoiced when Mother was able to go to church again. Though it took great effort for her to go she attended fairly regularly in good weather. On her not so good days Dad did not push her to go but let her decide whether she felt equal to going. Sitting still for the duration of a church service was too long for her and made it very difficult to start out walking again. So, we regularly took a walk to the back of the church, over to the steps and back again to give her a break. She felt quite self-conscious about this at first but accepted it as a necessity.

One Sunday Mother slept during most of the church service and was listless when she came home. Ervin Hershberger's were there for dinner and while we were eating she suddenly sort of dropped her head down. Her spoon dropped to the floor and her expression went blank for a moment. Then her head came up and she wanted to go ahead with eating. She was not aware that her spoon had dropped. She finished her dinner but was very groggy and listless the rest of the day. Dr. Martin presumed she had had a mini stroke.

At the time Mother was stricken Dad seemed to be in fairly good health, but before the year was out he too had had several light strokes, sometimes one side and then the other would be affected for several days. In December he had a heart spell that caused him to collapse in the guinea pig house. The following (verbatim) writing, apparently the beginning of a letter was found among Mother's things concerning this episode:

*"Eli fell in the pellet Hay truck on the 9th of December 1976. He was by himself and could not get out right away, finally he did get out and finished feeding pigs and when he came out to gas pump Daniel Miller was there Eli asked Daniel to come along with him to the house, his pants were wet from the water on the floor in the pig house."*

## The Later Declining Years

As time went on Dad had numerous light strokes, some affecting his speech, sometimes an arm or leg, and occasionally leaving him confused for a while. On of these occasions he related that when he felt something coming over him he asked God to stop it so that he could take care of Mother. God answered his prayer. Later Eli commented that he may not have been as resigned as he should have been when he prayed that prayer. Then he added that he does hope that Amanda would be taken home a short time before he, so that he could take care of her as long as she lived. Many times in conversation as well as in audible prayers he expressed gratitude that she did not have to lie in bed suffering all these years since her stroke.

In 1980 Dad's eyesight began to fail due to cataracts. Poor vision, shortness of breath and weakness compelled him to give up building martin houses. An example of his determination was a day when he was picking beans and wanted to finish out his row and fill his bucket. But his legs buckled under him and he rolled over in the bean patch. With a humorous twist Dad related the incident, "I tried to get up but I couldn't so I called for help. Then I sat there on the ground and filled my bucket the second time!"

With Dad's vision problem there was some question about him driving but he continued to take short drives. One trip to the doctor in Salisbury made me quite tense. Mother noticed that he was driving fast and commented about it and I was sure that his vision was not good enough to drive that fast rather than at his usual slow, steady speed. Dad explained, (Seller truck iss mir noch, und Ich vill nett havva ess err um mich rum gayt." (That truck is after me and I don't want it to go around me!") Another time he drove up over the walk at the church, something that had never happened before.

One windy day when we had gone to the doctor I had just washed my hair and they were very unruly. Mother looked at me and said "Du gucksht ess vonn do dairrich a shtorm gonga varsht." (You look as though you went through a storm.) Then she seemed embarrassed, held her hand over her mouth and added, "Vell Ich vase nett vie Ich gook, faliecht noch shlimmer." (Well I don't know how I look, maybe even worse.)

One Sunday Dad became quite ill with a high fever. Mother was very tense and went to the bedroom over and over, probably feeling helpless but wishing she could do something for him. In May 1980 he became very sick during the night and agreed that Mother should press the buzzer which had been installed at the head of the bed. Effie came down and summoned help. By that time Dad was unconscious and was taken to the hospital by ambulance. Lena said, "Mother looked so little and helpless lying there in bed when they took Dad out."

Dad's temperature registered 105 degrees when he was admitted to the hospital, the problem, pneumonia. He responded quickly to treatment and was discharged the following week. Mother was overjoyed to see him and commented about his lips being parched probably from his fever. "Oh, Ich denk nett," said Dad. "Ich hopp kay fever cott." (Oh, I guess not I didn't have any fever.) Obviously the nurses had not shared all information with him.

After Effie moved to Norman L. Yoder's (her sister Barbara's home) Paul Yoder's Ethel and Elmer Beachy's Orpha took turns at living in with Grandpas. One of them overheard Dad telling Mother one day that she's such a pretty woman. Mother laughed, "Do you really think that way?" He praised her some more and she said, "Well, I thought I would be older." He told her that her cheeks were still so rosy. She then gave God credit for her good looks. Another time when He was lifting her on the bed he said, "You're still a pretty heavy chunk." Then there were the times when Mother was discouraged or concerned lest there was unforgiven sin in her life and Dad lovingly reassured her that they were all covered and prayed with her. He conducted family worship as long as he was able.

By this time Mother's health was failing, she was no longer able to get up by herself and was quite confused at times. One Sunday when she had been very listless and confused Allen and Alma Miller Maust came to visit. With her chair right in front of Mother so she could understand her, Alma chatted about their school days. Mother became Alma's seat mate when she started to school and Alma was in second grade. They were seat mates the rest of Alma's school days.

Alma could recall only one occasion when they did not feel too kindly toward each other. They had found a picture that day that they both wanted and Mother had kept the picture. So Alma was not too happy. However she found an identical picture in a magazine at home that evening which she took along to school the next day and all was well between them again. She remembered sitting on the bank at school with Mother and singing at the tops of their voices. Her reminiscence made Mother's day. She brightened up amazingly, laughed and said, "Saug mir noch eppas ess Ich nimmy remember." (Tell me some more things that I don't remember.)

A very frustrating day for Mother was when she wanted an old apron brought from a room upstairs so that she could make something out of it. Try as they would no one could find the apron she described. Neither could this nonexistent room be found. Dear Mother cried in frustration because no one understood or believed what she was telling them. She was sure she could find it if she could only go upstairs. Dad offered to have Henry and Paul come over and carry her upstairs to look for it. But Mother did not want that.

Mother's confusion and wanting to go home had been somewhat frustrating to Dad. Then came the time when in his confusion he too wanted to go home. One Sunday evening they were both expressing their desire to go home and not stay "here" for the night. Then to my surprise Mother looked around the room and pointed out the fish aquarium and the clock with the bird in it as familiar objects that looked as though possibly?? they might be at home. But Dad knew better and wanted to go home for the night! However, Henry was able to persuade him to go to the bedroom with him where he pointed his bed out to him. Dad asked, "Iss sell my bett?" (Is that my bed?) Assured that it was he wanted to know, "Vare hutt dir's gasaught?" (Who told you?) but he willing got ready and went to bed then.

Dad was a caring man and he cared enough to share. When due to his poor vision he could no longer take care of his mail the family became aware of the some 230 organizations that were soliciting funds from him. Of these he was supporting some 50, some worthy causes and some not so worthy.

Cataract surgery was scheduled for Dad in April of 1982. But two days before the date he had another light stroke and it was postponed until May 19, 1982. His eye was slow in healing, nor did he have the remarkable results which most people have. This was quite a let down for him. From then on his health declined rapidly. In July he was hospitalized with heart problems. Although tests indicated improvement in his condition when he was discharged from the hospital he continued to lose ground after coming home. Now that he could no longer care for Mother or read he seemed to have lost the will to live and frequently expressed a desire to go home and be with the Lord.

Mother too was declining and no longer able to walk. The family felt that their parents really needed professional care. In answer to both Josie Steven's and the family's prayers, Josie, a very capable L.P.N., and the family were led together. Josie moved in and took

1932-33 Front L-R: Edna, Mabel, Lena, John. Back row: Elizabeth, Ernest, Paul, Henry.

L-R: Henry, Paul, Ernest, John holding Patsy.

48

1967 Eli and Amanda's 50th Wedding Eli and Amanda about 1956-7.
Anniversary.

1956 Eli with two of his early built Martin houses
and one of his father-in-law Sam Hershbergers.

Early 1940s. L-R: Edna, Elizabeth, Lena, Mabel.

Early 1940s. Front L-R: John, Eli, Amanda. Second row: Elizabeth, Lena, Mabel, Edna. Back: Ernest, Paul, Henry.

over their day care while family members took turns with night duty. Because of Mother's severe hearing loss and Dad's voice having dwindled to a mere whisper their only means of communication was by holding hands, which they enjoyed.

The children, with their companions celebrated their parent's 65th wedding anniversary with both of them in wheelchairs. Edna left her missionary duties in Haiti to come home for the occasion. After the open house for their 50th anniversary the family had concluded that there was nothing they could do for their parents that they would enjoy more than for the entire family to gather in their home to sing for them and it had become a family practice. Though the group was small on this day we sang for a short while. A favorite song of Dad's "Bay Denkie Mench Das Endie", which he had often selected and lead out in church services was sung and he was moved to tears.

Over the years Dad had shown interest in, and befriended the Fazenbaker children who lived in the trailer behind the plant. Occasionally he had sturdy Stevie help him with a difficult job and paid him for it. A few days before Christmas, Sandy, one of the Fazenbaker girls, brought candy for Dads' Christmas gift. Dad was bedfast, recuperating from pneumonia and not seeming to be aware of what was going on around him, and Mother was confused and unable to visit. So Sandy was heartily thanked but not invited in. After she was gone Dad expressed his concern that she should have been invited in and entertained. Perhaps he had a desire to see her once more.

## The Business Goes On

As Dad became more feeble he discontinued his guinea pig business, his daily rounds through the plant, and his involvement in the business. Then too, he distributed most of his shares to his children, thus making them shareholders in the corporation which had been formed in 1975. However, his interest and concern in the business remained keen and he desired to be kept informed of new developments. Even in 1991, eight years after Dad's passing, Henry finds himself thinking he should tell Dad about unusual happenings.

Open house on Labor Day 1990, when over 900 people registered, five tour guides were kept very busy all day showing people through the plant, and long lines of people waited to see the video of the Meat Packing Plant in operation, was a reminder of the continued growth of the business since Dad's home going. With a bit of imagination about what his reaction might have been had he returned for Open House one can visualize his obvious astonishment at the sight of the new offices, and smoke house as well as additional coolers, automatic equipment, and the slurry storage. Can't you almost hear his pleased chuckle at the report of the small beginning of his business in a shed on a farm in St. Paul, Pa., having grown into a modern Meat Packing Plant with 18 shareholders, hiring approximately 120 employees, slaughtering an average of over 4,000 animals a week, producing dozens of products and delivering to points in Pennsylvania, Maryland, Virginia, West Virginia, and Washington, D.C.?

## Dad's Home Going and Funeral

Dad became weaker and developed more problems, including congestive heart failure and pneumonia, which had responded to treatment but then he had a relapse. Dr. Martin said he could be taken to the hospital and put on machines but he did not advise it. And the family knew that Dad would not want that. On January 5, 1983, when Josie had the day off and Lena was with Dads he passed away at 5:15 p.m. This was the first death in the family since baby Elmer's unexpected death over 64 years earlier.

Since Edna had been home in October for their anniversary she did not come from Haiti for the funeral. Simon N. Schrock and Henry Tice brought the messages. Henry referred to the time Eli bought the Dr. Davis farm and expressed gratitude for what Eli had done. Henry is doubtful that his Uncle Eli had any idea of the impact his concern about this 11-year-old nephew of his had on him. He related that his parents were concerned about Eli going into debt to provide a home for them, but that was what he did. Henry expressed his appreciation to Dad concerning this just a few weeks before his death. Then too, he related that in the many years Eli Tice worked for Eli Yoder it was with the clear understanding that he should consider his church responsibilities as first ahead of any other work. It is Henry's opinion that the reason the Lord so richly blessed Eli's many business ventures was because they were for the service of others.

Mother seemed to be at least in part aware of what had happened. They took her in to see Dad before the undertaker arrived and she made some comment about glory?? Later in the evening she suggested that someone would need to make funeral arrangements. Other than that she was calm and quiet.

The day before Dad's passing Mother had said, "The angels are singing! The angels are singing. Don't you hear them?" Asked what they were singing she said, "They're coming, they're coming." The day following his death she could not be roused all day and her pulse dropped down into the 40s. At five o'clock she awoke and asked for supper. The rest of the evening she was quite confused but otherwise she seemed quite her usual self. The following day she asked why the angels did not come.

Mother was approached as to whether she would like to go to the morgue but she chose not to go, and the family along with Josie knew that it would not be advisable to take her to the funeral. Dear Josie took care of her that day. When someone came in after the funeral Mother asked "Is it all over now?" That evening she announced that her name is Amanda Hershberger, she is 12 or 13 years old and her best friend is Alma Miller.

## Mother's Last Months

Mother continued to decline and became so disoriented that it was difficult to know whether she was grieving for Dad. One day when she was making crying sounds Josie asked her whether she is grieving for Dad and she replied "Oh that was long ago." Another day Josie told her not to make those crying sounds. Mother looked at her searchingly and said "Well, I don't have anything else to do." As time went on she had good days, bad days and days when she slept practically all the time. Edna had inquired in a letter whether I think she remembers that she has a daughter Edna. So I tried to discover how much she does remember and asked her how many children she has. She said, "There are ten" and began to name Jonas B. Miller's family. Another day she might have named her own, without faltering.

In those last months there were times when she became very restless and singing with her seemed to relax her. One day she sang to the tune of "My Jesus I Love Thee," the words, "I think that I saw you when to heaven I fly," over and over again. When I tried to keep her occupied with a child's stack-em toy on a restless day she stacked the rings several times then she looked at me earnestly and announced "Ich conn nett saena ess sell gute iss fer ennick eppas may ess zeit ferdripe." (I can't see that that is good for a thing but to pass the time.)

Nights too varied a great deal with a rare night when she was quiet, so quiet that one went in to check and be sure she was all right. More often though she talked much of the night. It seemed that she was dreaming out loud. And as time went on the things she seemed to be doing in mind, receded farther and farther back into her life until she was calling people she knew in childhood.

Most often though she called Dad very very earnestly. Occasionally, had it not been so pathetic to have Mother so disoriented, it would have been very comical. One night Lena asked her whether she could close her eyes and go to sleep now. Pretty soon she was calling again, "Eli, Eli, Eli! you should close your eyes and go to sleep like I do!" Usually when we went in to check on her we would find her appearing to be asleep. One night when she repeatedly called and asked, "Iss der raum ready? Iss der raum ready?" (Is the cream ready?) I went in to check on her and she appeared to be sound asleep except for the repeated question.

In May she developed congestive heart failure and pneumonia. The last weeks she was in a semi-coma, able to swallow, but responding only a few times during that time. She passed away Sunday morning May 29, 1983, at 9:15 while Ernest and Elizabeth were with her. They phoned the message down to the Mt. View Church. Although there was sadness and sorrow in parting with both parents in so short a time the family rejoiced to see them released from their frail bodies and the frustrations they faced in their last years.

Edna came home from Haiti for the funeral, where Ervin Hershberger and Ivan J. Miller brought the messages. The following gem found in Mother's 1969 diary was read by Ervin at the funeral:

"Lord we thank you for your protection over us through the year of 1968 and all through our life so far. I am sorry for the mistakes I have made in so many different areas in my life, but I feel the Lord has forgiven me. Now, 1969 lies before us with a clean sheet. Lord, I ask for thy help and guidance for every day. Help me that I do not speak when I should be silent, and when I should speak give me the words that I should say, that they may be edifying. I ask for thy help from day to day for without Thee we can do no good thing."

# Lasting Impressions

Among lasting impressions which the children treasure were: Henry's distinct recollection of his mother turning to the little boys on the back of the spring wagon when they were going down the Bender Hill to a baptismal service at the Niverton Church and telling them to listen real good to the sermon that day.

Mother's parting words, "Put you trust in a Higher Power." when her three sons were leaving home to go with a large group of boys to Baltimore by train for their physical examinations challenged Henry.

A memory the children treasure is their mother's careful avoidance of bragging and her quiet but firm squelching of criticism by redirecting the critic to thinking of the good points of the one being criticized. Paul recalls bringing a report home from school that he thought was big enough and bad enough that even his mother should be impressed. But she quietly pointed out that the person may have had a good reason for doing what he did.

Over the years their parent's overwhelmingly generous gifts as well as their help has been deeply appreciated by the children. Claude and Edna especially appreciated their faithful support during their years in Haiti.

In retrospect, as a daughter-in-law I would like to say that the Yoder's were wonderful in-laws, always ready to help in any way possible, but never meddling into their children's affairs.

My father-in-law's demonstration of Christian integrity and friendly sensitivity to the people he dealt with won him many friends. Being of a somewhat quiet and reserved nature, his influence was more in deeds than in words. For example: his offering to return some money to a man whom he learned had lost money in a deal with him, impressed his sons as a practical example of the "Golden Rule." The four sons agreed that their father's staunch practice and example of honesty was more effective and far reaching than any amount of lecturing would have been.

I knew my mother-in-law as a quiet, uncomplaining and unassuming person, whose heart and hands reached out to others in many ways. Having lost my mother at the age of seven my mother-in-law was especially precious to me.

While it is true that our parents have gone to be with the Lord, our precious memories will linger and their Christian influence will live on for generations to come.

With the passing of Eli and Mandy Yoder, the Casselman Valley lost a loving benevolent couple who contributed much to its people as well as to its economy.

Nine years have passed since our parents were called home. Since then four family members have joined them. December 20, 1985 a tragic accident snuffed out the life of Marlin Schrock, and on Ernest's 63rd birthday May 16, 1986, while doing a kind deed for a neighbor girl, Ernest drowned in his beautiful farm pond. During 1985 Mabel developed hip trouble and in October the problem was diagnosed as multiple myloma. After more than a year of suffering through which (quoting a sister-in-law) "She became sweeter and sweeter," a brain tumor swiftly took it's toll. She went to be with the Lord July 21, 1987. April 5, 1992, Sheldon joined the Heavenly throng. Only God knows who will be next to leave the family circle.

(All spelling and punctuation of the following are as in the original. Eli was about 12 years old and said he never got farther than 4th grade.)

# Gems From Eli's 1908 Notebook

## The Cooney's

The coon is a wild animal in the woods. They like to be along the creeks in the woods. There body is just like the ground hog's is. All except it is broader, and their heads is pointy and their tail is long and bushy.

They sleep in the day and threw the night they are out and around. There home is a hollow tree or someplace like thet.

Some people goes out and hunts them in the summer and sometimes takes them home if the dog chases them up.

John Wanger's dog chased three of them up a little tree, and he got them down, and one of then died. We traded a bull dog for them. We made a big cage for then, outside our coal house and made a holl so they can run around in the boxes in the coal house. When we open the boxes they run in the other boxes. The other week a chicken died and we gave it to the coons. We held it in to them and they first layind as if they were fast asleep and all at once they made a jump and had it.

Papa could hardly get it out. They are just wild after the rats.

## George Washington

George Washington was born in Va. he was the president of the U.S.A When he was only 11 years old his father died. He went to school to learn reading and writeing. This is one of his verses he wrote in his copy book.

Labor to keep alive on your breast that little spark of celestial fire is called con-suice.

His mother had a nice little colt he was so wild that they couldn't catch him. So one morning George went out and some boys was there and he said, "Boys if you will get him in a corner I will ride him." And they got him in and George slipped up behing and put the bridle on and he got on.

The colt tried to get him of but he might just as well try to thro his own skin of as George. The colt jumped up on his hind feet and a blood tube bursted and he dropped down dead. He went in the house and told the whole story then his mother said that she would rather loos the flavored colt then have him tel a lie.

He always said the truth and never said a lie.

He was in a lot of battles and never got wounded, but there was two horses shot from under him and four bullets threw his coat.

George was a surveyer. He and Lord fairfax spent weeks together hunting Dear and foxes. His home was in Mount vern.

# The Young Entrepreneur

## Later Recordings in the 1908 Composition Book

| | | | | |
|---|---|---|---|---|
| Oct.1st. 1910 at 4 cents | $8.00 | | | |
| Nov. 1, 1911 at .04 cents | $9.00 | | | |
| 1911 to Inters. | .32 | Nov. 1, 1912 | .36 |
| 1911 to Inters. | .32 | Nov. 1, 1913 | .36 |
| Paid | .72 | | |
| 1912 to Inters. | .32 | | |
| 1913 to Inters. | .32 | | |
| Paid | .96 | | |

### Following is a record of salve and game sold:

Save Sold first dozen $1.00

| | | | | | |
|---|---|---|---|---|---|
| Monroe Yoder | 1 box | .25 | Miss Beachy | 1 box | .25 |
| Lewis Yoder | 1 box | .25 | Milt Yoder | 1 box | .25 |
| Mose Beachy | 1 box | .25 | Menno Beachy | 1 box | .25 |
| Miss Lee | 1 box | .25 | Uncle Johns | 1 box | .25 |

### Game 1913

| | | | | |
|---|---|---|---|---|
| 3 No. 4 skunks at | .40 | 1 No. 1 skunk one half my @ | $2.00 |
| 1 No. 2 opposum | .60 | 1 No. 1 skunk | 2.50 |

1 sqarrel read, 1 cat coalered, 1 weasle brown

### Expences from April 1910 to April 1911 '

| | | | | | |
|---|---|---|---|---|---|
| Apr. 8 | 1 trap | $0.05 | Apr.18 | 5 stamps | $0.05 |
| Apr. 25 | something in store | .03 | May 24 | 9 " | .09 |
| May 24 | 2 postals | .02 | June 2 | 1 bu. wheat | 1.00 |
| June 2 | 1 watch | .17 | July 2 | 1 box peanuts | .05 |
| July 4 | 1 box Peanuts | .05 | July 5 | 1/4 bu. wheat | .25 |
| July 6 | Postals | .01 | Aug. 13 | 10 stamps | .10 |
| Aug. 25 | 3 bananas | .05 | Aug. 25 | 1/4 bu. wheet | .25 |
| Sept.21 | 5 c. candy | .05 | Sept.29 | 2 enloved | .02 |
| Oct. 2 | 2 enlove | .02 | Nov. | Candy | .05 |
| Nov. 15 | some candy | .06 | Nov. | 2 traps | .48 |
| Nov. | bullets | .10 | Nov. | 1 rifle | 3.50 |

### 1911

| | | | | | |
|---|---|---|---|---|---|
| Jan. | 5 postals | .05 | Jan. 25 | Candy | .05 |
| Feb. 1 | 2 boxes caps | .01 | Feb. " | stamps | .08 |
| Feb.23 | Candy | .05 | Mar. 9 " | paper | .25 |
| Mar. 8 | getting gun fixed | .05 | " " " | money order | .03 |
| Apr. 1 | stamps | .07 | | | |
| Total | | $6.63 | | | |

### My Income 1910 - 11

| | | | |
|---|---|---|---|
| June 13 | to | 2 rosters | $0.83 |
| July 5 | " | 5 chickens 55 C. a piece | 2.75 |
| Sept. | " | 2 rosters breader | 1.75 |

| Sept. | " | 1 rat caught | .02 |
| Nov. | " | 100 lbs. iron | .35 |
| Nov. | " | 1 skunk hide | .10 |
| Dec. | " | 1 Mink hide | 3.00 |

## 1911

| | | | |
|---|---|---|---|
| Jan. | " | killing rats | .05 |
| " | " | some hides, (cat & calf) | .35 |
| " | " | taking buggy home | .25 |
| Feb. | " | catching rats | .08 |
| Mar. 30 | " | Postals | .17 |
| | | | $9.77 |

## Cousin Cards

Following are two post cards addressed to Eli:

April 22, 1914, "Dear Cousin I got your card alright I know what you are after you thought we would call him Eli you wanted to remind us of your name. Mail Written in a hurry, Cousin Sadie Hershberger. Come out on Sunday and give him a name."

April 24, 1914, "Dear Cousin—As we obeyed to your advise I think you are in entitled to get a dress for the little boy. We named him according to your instructions thanks for same Mam said if you would rather wait till he is bigger and then get a coat and pans for him that would do ha ha. Cousin"
(These were obviously from Sadie Hersberger, Mrs. Elmer Schrock when her brother Ervin Hersberger was a baby. Ervin was not aware that Eli had any influence in naming him, but here is the evidence.)

## INTERESTING ITEMS AND COSTS OF PURCHASES IN 1919

| | | | |
|---|---|---|---|
| 1. kettle | $0.70 | 1. extension table | $16.25 |
| 1. Coal Box | .10 | 92 1/2 bu. coal @ .07 | 6.48 |
| 1. gross clothes pins | .59 | 1. bread riser | 2.00 |
| 1. egg beater | .12 | 1. potato masher | .25 |
| 1. rolling pin | .10 | 1. cake turner | .05 |
| 1. potato slicer | .10 | My name on mailbox | .75 |
| 2 small pans | .20 | 1 lantern | 1.50 |
| 1 sewing machine | 25.00 | 1 lawn mower | 7.10 |
| 1 corner shonk | 7.10 | 1 pup | 1.50 |

Possibly some of the above items were bought at an auction for one entry says "a pan and some other trash."

No indication of Henry's arrival shows up in Nov. 1919 but Dec. 5 lists a baby crib. $11.95

Frequent recordings of maid labor indicate that Dad's had a maid while living on the Fisher farm.

February of 1920 records: dressing finger three times $5.00 evidently the time Dad lost his finger in the grinder. Then February 21 lists a doctor's charge of $9.25 . Question, was this an additional charge for the care of the finger or might it have been the delivery fee for Henry??

July 27, 1920 lists 1. cream separator $125.00

April 21,1921, shoes & rubbers for Henry 1.65

August 28,1921, Dr. Bill 25.00. This obviously was the delivery fee for Paul. No other delivery fees show up in ledgers.

| | | | |
|---|---|---|---|
| 1. wash machine | $48.50 | 12. cakes soap | $0.94 |
| 1. bbl. flour | 15.25 | 1. hand wagon | 4.00 |
| 6 tin cups wild indigo | .30 | dog tax | 1.00 |

## Additional 1920 and 1921 Expenses

| | | | |
|---|---|---|---|
| 100 lbs, sugar | 18.00 | Suspenders | .50 |
| 2. plum trees | 2.00 | Oct. thrashing | 28.21 |
| 1. hat | .50 | 1. buggy | 15.00 |
| 1. Baby high chair | 4.00 | 1. Pitcher pump | 5.25 |

## 1921

| | | | |
|---|---|---|---|
| renewing Republican | 5.00 | 1. broom | .65 |
| 5. lbs. rice | 1.00 | 3. yds. oilcloth | 1.50 |
| 1 bu. peaches | 1.00 | 6. pr. socks | .75 |

## Some prices in the early years

Crackers .22, Sausage .28,     veal and mutton .20, sausage .28, sugar .11, and ham and beef .35 cents a pound. Potatoes were .75, coal .07 a bu., apple butter $1.50, Kerosene .16 -.17 a gal., Hay $3.00 a ton and 50 lbs. of flour, $3.35.

## Egg and butter prices 1919 to 1928 and 1931 to 1933

| Year | Eggs | Butter |
|---|---|---|
| 1919 | 32 to 65 cents a doz. | 40 to 65 cents a pound |
| 1920 | 30 to 75 | 55 to 65 |
| 1921 | 25 to 76 | 34 to 60 |
| 1923 | 40 to 57 | 30 to 52 |
| 1924 | 25 to 35 | 40 to 45 |
| 1926 | 28 to 69 | 40 to 45 |
| 1927 | 25 to 63 | 30 to 55 |
| 1928 | 24 to 50 | 35 to 50 |
| 1931 | 11 to 28 | 25 to 30 |
| 1932 | 13 to 37 | 16 to 25 |
| 1933 | 11 to 27 | 20 to 25 |

## Eli Yoder's Diary of Daily Happenings in 1926

JANUARY 1926

| | | |
|---|---|---|
| Jan. | 1 | At home. |
| Sat. | 2 | Fetched cow from Tice's sale |
| Sun. | 3 | At Lewis Yoders also Simons. |
| Mon. | 4 | Butchered, Menno and Jonas and Kate P. helped. |

| | | |
|---|---|---|
| Tues. | 5 | At Frank Yutzy's sale. |
| Wed. | 6 | In church at Niverton |
| Thur. | 7 | Went to Yutzy for wagon |
| Fri. | 8 | Dug coal and worked at barn. |
| Sat. | 9 | Cleaned chicken houses |
| Sun. | 10 | In church at Niverton |
| Mon. | 11 | In Salisbury and at John Ds. for dinner |
| Tues. | 12 | Mixed chicken feed and cleaned house |
| Wed. | 13 | hauled manure |
| Thur. | 14 | dug coal and hauled them up - Amanda at Jones |
| Fri. | 15 | hauling manure |
| Sat. | 16 | Fetched feed from Schrocks and cleaned stables |
| Sun. | 17 | At Alberts, also Clarences were there |
| Mon. | 18 | Cleaning stables, raining most of the time. |
| Tues. | 19 | Lined cowstable door, manured strawberries. |
| Wed. | 20 | Butter and eggs to town, Bees flying all day |
| Thur. | 21 | Putting manure at raspberry plants |
| Fri. | 22 | In church at Summit Mills very stormy |
| Mon. | 23 | Out for egg cases and maid for Simons |
| Tues. | 24 | Cleaned chicken house and worked at barn. |
| Wed. | 25 | To Meyersdale, snowing and blowing |
| Thur. | 26 | Working in barn, zero weather |
| Fri. | 27 | Made bill out for brooder house, to Salisbury |
| Sat. | 28 | Fetched J.K. Beilers from Salisbury, cleaned stables |
| Fri. | 29 | Put bath room door on, near zero, blowing |
| Sat. | 30 | Dug coal and hauled manure on strawberries |
| Sun. | 31 | At home Amanda at Simons P.M. |

## FEBRUARY 1926

| | | |
|---|---|---|
| Mon. | 1 | |
| Tues. | 2 | |
| Wed. | 3 | Jonas Tice and I digging coal |
| Thur. | 4 | (deep snow) to Coal Run this PM to sell Rose & butter |
| Fri. | 5 | At Simons A.M. took Beilers to Abe Kinsingers P.M. |
| Sat. | 6 | Sorted keelers and took them to Meyersdale for repairs. |
| Sun. | 7 | All in church at Niverton (Good sledding) |
| Mon. | 8 | Jonas and I digging coal (6 cars) |
| Tues. | 9 | 8 cars |
| Wed. | 10 | Butchered Rose and delivered her |
| Thur. | 11 | Menno fetched feed, I worked up quarter of beef. |
| F-S | 12-13 | Jonas Tice and I digging coal (6 cars both days.) |
| Sun. | 14 | Sunday evening we went at Sam Hershbergers |
| Mon. | 15 | Came home from Hershbergers |
| Tues. | 16 | Went to Meyersdale got flooring and keelers |
| Wed. | 17 | Fetched load lumber at Amos Yoders |
| Thur. | 18 | Got silo staves riped, planted posts for brooder house |
| Fri. | 19 | Took Piney and small heifer to Hays |
| Sat. | 20 | took oats to Jonas Tice, ground it to horse sale Meyersdale |
| Sun. | 21 | In church, Summit, N.M. Yoder's youngsters here for dinner |
| Mon. | 22 | Scalded keelers (Snow left rapidly) |
| Tues. | 23 | To Salisbury get spiles, auger & set up plow, Pauh here |
| Wed. | 24 | hauled keelers, taped in afternnon, our side |

| Thur. | 25 | Fetched roofing and hauled sugar water |
|---|---|---|
| Fri. | 26 | At Jake Folk's sale. Menno hauled sugar water |
| Sat. | 27 | Stirring off and went to Meyersdale |
| Sun. | 28 | At home all day nobody here. Menno and Tillie at Sammies. |

## MARCH 1926

| Mon. | 1 | Moved brooder house, taped Jackson trees hauled, 15 bbl. |
|---|---|---|
| Tues. | 2 | hauled 13 b. sugar water, plowed chick yard |
| Wed. | 3 | To Meyersdale got water fountains, butter and eggs |
| Thur. | 4 | Cleaned chicken house, repairing table, harness |
| Fri. | 5 | Stirring off, fetched Kansas doe in Meyersdale |
| Sat. | 6 | Fetched young bull at Sam Hershbergers |
| Sun. | 7 | Church at Niverton. Annie Beachy for dinner |
| Mon. | 8 | Menno worked at barn, Jake and Susie Petersheim here for dinner |
| Tues. | 9 | Putting in water fountains, Menno in town |
| Wed. | 10 | Dressed 7 hogs at Wengerd, throwed ice out in keelers |
| Thur. | 11 | Menno in town, I framed brooder house |
| Fri. | 12 | In Meyersdale, Menno hauling manure |
| Sat. | 13 | I framed brooder house, Menno hauling manure |
| Sun. | 14 | At home, Tillie and I at John Hostetler this afternoon |
| Mon. | 15 | Building brooder house |
| Tues. | 16 | Butcherd 6 hogs for Wenger, Menno fetched feed |
| Wed. | 17 | At sale at Gnagey farm, Menno hauling manure |
| Thur. | 18 | Working at brooder house (sugar water started) |
| Fri. | 19 | At Gnagey's sale, Menno hauled 35 b. sugar water |
| Sat. | 20 | hauled sugar water, boiled it out (19 b.) |
| Sun. | 21 | At Sarah Hostetlers furnel in afternoon |
| Mon. | 22 | Cleaned chicken house, Menno hauled 15 b. sugar water |
| Tues. | 23 | Plowed and hauled sugar water (15 b.) |
| Wed. | 24 | butcher beef, S.H. stirred off, Menno plowed |
| Thur. | 25 | Took syrup in Salisbury |
| Fri. | 26 | In Meyersdale, set up small brooder |
| Sat. | 27 | At Sol Hostetler, killed heafer, cleaned brooder house |
| Sun. | 28 | At home Noah Beachy, Fred Millers here for dinner |
| M-T | 29-30 | Hauled water and manure, retaped some Tues. |
| Wed. | 31 | to Salisbury fetched chicks, Menno hauled 40 b. sugar water |

## APRIL 1926

| Thur. | 1 | Fetched fertilizer and brooder, took butter to town |
|---|---|---|
| Fri. | 2 | At home (Good Friday) Effie and Barbara were here |
| Sat. | 3 | Hauling sugar water, stirring off (50 b.) |
| Sun. | 4 | I was in church, Amanda at home (Easter) |
| Mon. | 5 | At home all day nobody here |
| Tues. | 6 | hauling sugar water 50 b. |
| Wed. | 7 | Throwed ice out of keelers, stirred off, to Salisbury |
| Thur. | 8 | hauled sugar water and made syrup 50 b. |
| Fri. | 9 | Fetched feed at Niverton, took butter to town |
| Sat. | 10 | Putting sheating on chick house |
| Sun. | 11 | At home all day, Amnada was sick. |
| Mon. | 12 | Boiled sugar water and worked at brooder house |
| Tues. | 13 | Working at brooder house |
| Wed. | 14 | Worked at brooder house and fetched chicks |

| Thur. | 15 | Cleaned out chicken coup worked on chicks |
| Fri. | 16 | Menno plowed I was in Meyersdale |
| Sat. | 17 | Hauled sugar water, cleaned up |
| Sun. | 18 | All in church at Summit, Sams here for dinner |
| Mon. | 19 | plowing, snowing part of the time. |
| Tues. | 20 | Plowing with tractor above orchard |
| Wed. | 21 | Fetched chicks and was in Salisbury |
| Thur. | 22 | Fetched brooder set it up put chicks out |
| Fri. | 23 | Was in Meyersdale with butter and eggs |
| Sat. | 24 | Cleaned chick houses, sowed bottom in oats. |
| Sun. | 25 | At home all day no body here |
| Mon. | 26 | To Jonas Tice for oil and chopper and hauled rocks |
| T-W | 27-28 | Harrowed with tractor at Speichers |
| Thur. | 29 | Plowed potatoe piece and harrowed it |
| Fri. | 30 | Sowed oats at Speichers ˙ |

## MAY 1926

| Sat. | 1 | In Meyersdale and fetched potatoes at N.J.K. |
| Sun. | 2 | In church at Niverton, back for dinner |
| Mon. | 3 | In Berlin and Somerset, bought tractor |
| Tues. | 4 | Planted potatoes |
| Wed. | 5 | Hauled load of hay |
| Thur. | 6 | In Meyersadale with butter and eggs |
| F-S | 7-8 | Plowing for corn at Speichers in P.M. |
| Sun. | 9 | In church at Niverton, back home for dinner |
| Mon. | 10 | Got corn field ready for planting at Speichers |
| Tues. | 11 | Went to Somerset for repairs and bee supplies |
| Wed. | 12 | Planted corn at Speichers |
| Thur. | 13 | at home, Menno to Cumberland to see Sarah |
| Fri. | 14 | harrowed and grinded oats |
| Sat. | 15 | Planted silage corn, mangles and sweet corn |
| Sun. | 16 | In church at Summit, Noah Beachys here for dinner |
| Mon. | 17 | Cleaned chicken house, cleaned up manure |
| Tues. | 18 | |
| Wed. | 19 | Working on bees |
| Thur. | 20 | Took cattle up in pasture then at M.M.Bs. |
| Fri. | 21 | In Meyersdale and digging post holes |
| Sat. | 22 | Working at orchard fence |
| Sun. | 23 | In church at Niverton, back for dinner |
| Sun. | 24 | All at home, Franie Hostetler here |
| Mon. | 25 | To Salisbury and Springs for feed |
| Wed. | 26 | Worked at bees, worked at orchard fence |
| Thur. | 27 | Put roost in for chicks took brooder out |
| Fri. | 28 | In Meyrsdale |
| Sat. | 29 | Worked at bees, fetched wheat at S. Hostetlers |
| Sun. | 30 | In church at Niverton, at Noah Hershbergers-dinner |
| Mon. | 31 | At Sam H. Sun night at M.M.Bs. in P.M. |

## JUNE 1926

| Tues. | 1 | working at manure pit (scooping) |
| Wed. | 2 | Worked at bees and manure pit, hauled sand |
| Thur. | 3 | to Niverton & Ben Fishers for cement mixer and sand |

| Fri. | 4 | Menno fetched cement & to Meyersdale P.M. Louie Beachy here for dinner |
|------|---|------|
| Sat. | 5 | Putting up form for manure pit |
| Sun. | 6 | at home- Jonas T. in Oakland their kids stay here |
| Mon. | 7 | working at manure pit |
| Tues. | 8 | finished form, hauling stone and sand |
| Wed. | 9 | cemented pit and a little in pig pen |
| Thur. | 10 | made fence and started plowing corn |
| Fri. | 11 | to Meyersdale & Salisbury, team, fetched feed |
| Sat. | 12 | plowing corn, orchard field |
| Sun. | 13 | In church at Summit Old Folks here for dinner |
| Mon. | 14 | At Len Mausts cut queen cells out, hauled sand |
| Tues. | 15 | Menno fetched egg cases, washed church house |
| Wed. | 16 | Put supers on bees, got feeding room ready to cement |
| Thur. | 17 | cemented floor of manure pit & feeeding room |
| Fri. | 18 | In Meyersdale, got swarm of bees at Len Mausts |
| Sat. | 19 | Worked at bees (supers on) and plowed corn |
| Sun. | 20 | At home, Milt Benders here at 6 o'clock |
| Mon. | 21 | finished corn at Normans, broilers to Clarences |
| Tues. | 22 | In Somerset for bee supplies |
| Wed. | 23 | Worked on bees A.M. , planted cabbage |
| Thur. | 24 | In Meyersdale, fetched load of hay |
| Fri. | 25 | worked on bees A.M. plowed |
| Sat. | 26 | Put screens in windows cleaned brooder house |
| Sun. | 27 | In church at Niverton, Clarences for dinner |
| M-T | 28-29 | Mowed and plowed corn |
| Wed. | 30 | Shocked hay, put one load in |

## JULY 1926

| Thur. | 1 | In Meyersdale also picked strawberries |
|------|---|------|
| Fri. | 2 | Planted cabbage from Zook and put in 2 loads of hay |
| Sat. | 3 | plowed potatoes,corn put in rakens |
| Sun. | 4 | At N.J. Kinsingers all day |
| Mon. | 5 | I was at M.M. Beachys, Sam Ys. Helmuths, got supers |
| Tues. | 6 | mowed yard worked in strawberry patch |
| Wed. | 7 | shipped 10 giant hens from Meyersdale |
| Thur. | 8 | Picked strawberries, planted cabbage, at Joe Wengerd's funrel |
| Fri. | 9 | took 300 roosters to Summit Hotel |
| Sat. | 10 | worked at bees, cleaned raspberry patch |
| Sun. | 11 | church at Summit, Emanuel and Katie H. here-dinner |
| Mon. | 12 | At Grandie's furnel at Maple Glen House |
| Tues. | 13 | In church at Summit Will and Iddo preached |
| Wed. | 14 | In Manges piece (Cleaning) |
| Thur. | 15 | Butcherd Sandy |
| Fri. | 16 | In Meyersdale and plowed corn |
| Sat. | 17 | Menno plowed I cleaned raspberry patch |
| Sun. | 18 | At home A.M. at Gid's P.M. (Was this the day Ernest smelled Candy?) |
| Mon. | 19 | Picking cherries and raspberries |
| Tues. | 20 | took raspberries to Salisbury and at A. Hostetler sale |
| Wed. | 21 | Mowed grass and picked cherries |
| Thur. | 22 | Mowed, took cherries to Salisbury, cut John Hostetler's wheat |

| | | |
|---|---|---|
| Fri. | 23 | In Meyersdale, picked raspberries |
| Sat. | 24 | At S. Hostetler got wheat, got some hay in |
| Sun. | 25 | I at church in Niverton, nobody here for dinner |
| Mon. | 26 | Picked raspberries and took them to town |
| Tues. | 27 | Cut wheat at Speichers |
| Wed. | 28 | through Sat. 31 making hay and picking raspberries |

## AUGUST 1926

| | | |
|---|---|---|
| Sun. | 1 | |
| Mon. | 2 | through Wed. 4. Making hay and picking raspberries |
| Thur. | 5 | Put in hay and mowed the last |
| Fri. | 6 | Picked raspberries and took to Meyersdale |
| Sat. | 7 | Worked bee supplies and went to Jonas Tices, P.M. |
| Sun. | 8 | All at home |
| Mon. | 9 | Finished making hay |
| Tues. | 10 | Finished wheat and started digging potatoes |
| Wed. | 11 | digging early potatoes |
| Thur. | 12 | Plowing for wheat |
| Fri. | 13 | thrashed wheat and started cutting oats.. |
| Sat. | 14 | cutting oats , moved brooder house for rabbits |
| Sun. | 15 | all at home, church at Niverton |
| Mon. | 16 | Menno plowing, I worked at bees, picked cherries |
| Tues. | 17 | Plowed and took spring wagon at Kinsingers |
| Wed. | 18 | Worked at bees, made posts |
| Thur. | 19 | Tingering at barn, At Sam Yoders, Bought pullets |
| Fri. | 20 | Menno in Meyersdale, I picked sweet pippin |
| Sat. | 21 | |
| Sun. | 22 | At home, others in church at Niverton |
| M-W | 23-25 | plowing and making posts |
| Thur. | 26 | Cutting oats at Gids. |
| Fri. | 27 | Cutting oats in Speicher field |
| Sat. | 28 | Cutting oats in Speicher field at Gids |
| Sun. | 29 | At home, others in upper settlement |
| Mon. | 30 | Fetched 2 heafers from pasture |
| Tues. | 31 | Cutting oats for John Hostetler |

## SEPTEMBER 1926

| | | |
|---|---|---|
| Wed. | 1 | Took care of the little GIRL (Edna) |
| Thur. | 2 | tore the old fences out with the tractor |
| Fri. | 3 | Menno in town, I cleaned brooder house, tore shot cherry tree out |
| Sat. | 4 | Burning up big cherry tree |
| Sun. | 5 | All at home, church at Summit Mills, Sam H. here. |
| Mon. | 6 | burning brush went up at Dads for roosters |
| Tues. | 7 | Cut brush along upper fence. |
| W-T | 8-9 | |
| Fri. | 10 | Floyd Bender and I to Pinto for peaches |
| Sat. | 11 | Put away oats from Speicher's fields |
| Sun. | 12 | |
| M-T | 13-14 | put in oats out of bottom |
| W-T | 15-16 | Cutting corn for Jonas Tice |
| Fri. | 17 | Filled silo at Jonas Tice Sat. 18. sowed wheat |
| Sun. | 19 | I in church, Amanda and baby home, Claudes here for dinner |

64

| | | |
|---|---|---|
| Mon. | 20 | Started to cut corn at Speichers, worked on fence |
| T-W | 21-22 | Cutting corn for Simon Beachy |
| Thur. | 23 | Working at fence, helped Monroe fill silo |
| Fri. | 24 | In Meyersdale, dug post holes |
| Sat. | 25 | Fixing belts and chicken house for old hens |
| Sun. | 26 | All at home |
| Mon. | 27 | Cutting Gid's corn |
| Tues. | 28 | Cutting Gid's corn and started ours |
| Wed. | 29 | Filling silo at Gids |
| Thur. | 30 | Cutting our corn for silo |

OCTOBER 1926

| | | |
|---|---|---|
| Fri. | 1 | Filling our silo |
| Sat. | 2 | refilling silo and went to Meyersdale |
| Sun. | 3 | Church at Summit Mills, Daddie and Jake Zooks here for dinner |
| Mon. | 4 | Refilled silo here and at Gids |
| Tues. | 5 | Filled S.S. Hostetler's silo |
| Wed. | 6 | morning fetched heafer from pasture, P.M. at meeting |
| Thur. | 7 | church at Niverton - the preachers here |
| Fri. | 8 | Cut corn for Longs |
| Sat. | 9 | Cut corn for Malen Yoders |
| Sun. | 10 | All at home, Annie and Effie here after church |
| Mon. | 11 | |
| Tues | 12 | I worked at fence, Menno helped fill silo at Chaines |
| Wed. | 13 | helped thrash Monroes Buckwheat, planted posts |
| Thur. | 14 | through Sat. 16. |
| Sun. | 17 | In church at Summit, Clarences here for dinner |
| M-T | 18-19 | working at fence |
| Wed. | 20 | Made 2 gates for new fence |
| Thur. | 21 | Made steps for front porch and went to Meyersdale |
| F-S | 22-23 | Hauled in corn |
| Sun. | 24 | At home, John Zooks here |
| M-T | 25-26 | |
| Wed. | 27 | Gathered apples for apple butter |
| Thur. | 28 | Helped Jonas Tice at chicken house and to Kretchman's sale |
| Fri. | 29 | mowed weeds off potatoes got in 1 load cabbage |
| Sat. | 30 | Picking apples |
| Sun. | 31 | In church at Summit |

NOVEMBER 1926

| | | |
|---|---|---|
| Mon. | 1 | hunting rabbits and put in cabbage |
| Tues. | 2 | Dug potatoes and put in mangles |
| Wed. | 3 | At Speicher's sale |
| T-F | 4-5 | |
| Sat. | 6 | picked apples and dug potatoes |
| Sun. | 7 | At Ezra Yoders at Sam Hershbergers overnight |
| Mon. | 8 | Came back from Sam H. and dug potatoes |
| Tues. | 9 | dug potatoes and cleaned chicken house |
| Wed. | 10 | Hauling mangles |
| Thur. | 11 | In Meyersdale, opened silo |
| Fri. | 12 | At Jonas Tices working on chicken house |
| Sat. | 13 | ?????? In church at Niverton. |

```
S-S        14-20
Sun.       21   at home Noah Beachys and Ida Yoder here
Mon.       22   Butchered for ourself and Peck
Tues.      23   At Norman Gnagey's sale
Wed.       24   In Meyersdale
Thur.      25   In church at Niverton
Fri.       26   Butchered at Wengerds -
Sat.       27   At Salisbury & up home with Effie
Sun.       28   In church at Niverton
Mon.       29   Hunting rabbits and plowing
Tues.      30   Butchering at Bodes

DECEMBER 1926
Wed.        1   Killed beef for Speicher and to Meyersdale
T-S        2-4
Sun.        5   At home nobody here
Mon.        6   Out for deer
Tues.       7   Hauling manure
Wed.        8   In Salisbury and Meyersdale -
Thur.       9   Hauling manure took Piney away
```
The End - the rest is blank

# Records From the Late 20s

BROODERS SOLD IN 1926

Seniors at $28.12 to: Rudy Yoder, Floyd Yoder, Jacob Zook, Sam Zook, T.C.
   Beachy (Jennings) Shem Peachey, J.W. Speicher (Accident) Eli L. Yoder, Mon-
   roe Yoder, Lydia Bender, Ed Yoder, Eli L. Yoder, John Wengerd, Milt Yoder
   Enos Maust, Menno Yoder

Juniors at $22.50 to: Arthur Eichorn, J.W.Speicher, Lydia Bender, J.M.Yoder, M.W.
   Kinsinger (Somerfield, Pa.) C.H. Bird (Addison, Pa.) Joel Maust, Evan Miller

Total 24

BROODERS SOLD IN 1927

Seniors @ $28.12 to: Lewis Yoder, John D. Yoder, S.J. Miller, Sam Zook,2 to Fred
   Folk, Simon Orendorf, Norman Miller, Clarence Yoder

Juniors @ $22.50 to: Claude Yoder, Bennie Fisher, Aaron Miller, Myron Miller,
   O.R.Bender, Lela Brenneman, Byron Bender, J.M. Kauffman, Wm. Winterburg, Charley Easter, Lloyd Hay

Total 22

Business in 1928 & 29 dropped to a total of only 14 for the two years.

Mar. 5, 1931 records profit on 3 brooders to have been $7.11

RABBITS SOLD IN 1926

Does sold from $3.00 to $10.00 each - bucks from $1.50 to $4.50 each. They were
   shipped as far as Kalona, Iowa, Canada, Florida, Indiana and Norfolk, Va.
   Andy and Elmer Herhberger from Va. bought a Doe for $7.00 and a buck for
   $1.50. Total rabbit sales in 1926 were $633.47

1927 Cavie prices were 3 males for $1.96 females $1.00 each

1931 price .17 to .75 cents each

1927 BUTCHER HOUSE (or shed)

| | | |
|---|---|---|
| Sept. 2 | 6 bbl. cement @ $2.50 | $14.00 |
| Sept. 3 | Labor to make wall | 2.50 |
| | and tare shanty down | 3.35 |
| Sept. 13 | furnise front plate and ring | 8.00 |
| Oct. | Nails and spikes | 3.04 |
| Oct. | Brick and sand and lime | 19.70 |
| | roofing | 19.25 |
| | Lumber and windows | 8.60 |
| | labor for furnise | 8.00 |
| | | $76.44 |

# Records from the 30s

BUTCHER HOUSE 1932
BUILDING

| | |
|---|---|
| Blocks and bricks | $96.00 |
| 15 1/2 bbl. cement | 34.00 |
| Boalts and spikes | 1.75 |
| Windows and doors | 61.39 |
| Lumber for roof | 36.21 |
| Roofing | 50.00 |
| Labor (Charlie & Wm.) | 55.00 |
| | 7.50 |
| Paper Roll shelfs | 5.00 |

EQUIPMENT

| | |
|---|---|
| Pipes and Valves | $ 5.00 |
| Grinder bine | 20.00 |
| Boiler | 20.00 |
| Kettles | 10.00 |
| Engine | 10.00 |
| Track | 6.00 |
| Stuffer | 11.50 |
| Meat grinder | 7.00 |
| Bitts & grinder equip. | 5.00 |

| | |
|---|---|
| Building | $368.35 |
| Equipment | $99.00 |
| Total | $467.35 |

HOG STABLE COSTS 193?

| | |
|---|---|
| Lumber | $ 90.00 |
| 8 bbl. cement | 17.60 |
| Nails and spikes | 4.52 |
| Plaining and lumber and | |
| = 2X4 $2.00 | 9.40 |
| 4 bbl. cement @2.20 | $8.80 |
| 2 1/2 bbl. cement | 5.50 |
| 1 1/2 "   " | 3.30 |
| 10 windows 1 frame | 17.00 |
| Glutz Labor | $339.80 |
| Putting on roofing and spouting | |
| 1000ft. boards and labor to floor | |
| Total | 682.15 |
| | +26.00 |
| | 708.15 |
| | +21.00 |
| Total | $729.00 |

| | |
|---|---|
| Pipes and fittings | |
| Nails and bolts | $1.15 |
| 5 tn sand 1 tn stone | 6.25 |
| | 23.60 |
| 4 loads stone & sand | 5.00 |
| hinges/pipe fittings | 4.75 |
| Lumber for doors | 4.80 |
| Charlie Labor | 12.00 |
| | 74.63 |
| | 28.00 |

# GEMS FROM ELI'S LATER LEDGER 1933 TO 1944

May 1933 produce sold -.45 a bu., lard .07 a lb., butter .20 a lb., eggs .12 a doz.
Oct. 1933 sold 125 lbs. cabbage for $1.25
Nov. 25, 1933 sold 1438 lbs. cabbage @ $10.50
" " " " 2424 lbs. " `.18 a hundred $21.80

EXPENSE

| ? on date evidently 1932 | New Tractor | $1079.00 |
|---|---|---|
| June 1933 | Shoes for Eli | 3.50 |
| Dec. 1933 | Subscription to Poultry Tribune | 1.00 |
| Jan. 27, 1934 | Glasses for Lizzie | 10.00 |
| Aug. 1934 | Glasses for Paul and Edna | 23.00 |
| Dec. 24, 1934 | traded 1926 Dodge on 1931 Dodge Allowed $75.00 paid | $365.00 |
| March 1935 | Kitchen Cabinet | 12.85 |
| April 1935 | Pulling Amanda's 6 teeth | 4.50 |
| April 20, 1935 | Set of teeth for Eli | 24.00 |
| Aug. 1935 | 9 gal. huckleberries at.50 | 4.50 |
| Aug. 13 | Repair Paul's glasses | 5.25 |
| Oct. 1935 | 1/2 interest in corn binder (new) | 60.00 |
| June 1936 | 23,000 cabbage plants | 26.25 |
| June 1937 | 13,000 " " | 14.00 |
| Oct. 1939 | Making Paul's suit | 20.16 |
| Dec. 3,1939 | Tillie's wages | 251.70 |
| May 1940 | Case Tractor and Cultivator | 725.00 |
| May 1940 | Electric bill for two months | 8.49 |
| Sept. 9,1944 | Goods for Paul's suit | 12.68 |
| May. 7, 1942 | V MM Tractor | 1350.00 |
| Sept. 9,193? | 9 bu. peaches @ 1.00 | 9.00 |

Pages 140 &41 of this ledger record dental payment for all except
John of children.

Pages 50 to 52 record the strawberry crop of 1934.
Total sales- 10,362 quarts - Profit $607.30

## ITEMS FROM ELI'S 1940s LEDGERS

LEDGER 1941

| March | | Labor Fannie Kinsinger | $ 57.00 |
|---|---|---|---|
| Jan. | 15 | Driver's liscence for Ernest | 2.25 |
| Sept. | 3 | 1/3 share Case Thrasher | 333.00 |
| Oct. | 2 | National Sewing Machine | 85.00 |
| Oct. | 14 | 1/2 ton Dodge Pickup | 755.00 |
| Oct. | 14 | Ice Cream Freezer | 9.95 |
| Dec. | 2 | 1/3 share corn cutter | 100.00 |
| Dec. | 16 | Mennonite Publishing House | 16.56 |
| Dec. | 31 | 26 ton sweet corn (sold) | 283.00 |
| 1942 | | | |
| Feb. | 17 | Nash Sedan | $400.00 |
| Apr. | 2 | Barn Equipment | 360.00 |

| June | 25 | Blocks, sand, gravel laying barn wall | 278.00 |
|------|----|---------------------------------------|--------|
| July | 10 | Tractor and Mower repairs | 140.00 |
| Sept. | 28 | Windows for Milk House | 21.00 |
| Oct. | 5 | Pea Check (Peas sold) | 761.34 |
| Nov. | 6 | Blocks for Milk House | 79.32 |
| Dec. | 15 | Corn Check (Corn Sold) | 263.00 |

December 1942
Labor for Raymond $50.00
Labor for Paul $170.00
Labor for Henry $450.00

An age and weight record of the family about 1941, probably a report needed to get sugar when it was rationed, follows:

| Name | Age | Weight | Eyes | Hair | Height |
|------|-----|--------|------|------|--------|
| Henry | 22 | 135 | Brown | Brown | 5' 4" |
| Paul | 20 | 140 | " | " | 5' 5" |
| Ernest | 18 | 148 | " | " | 5' 7" |
| Elizabeth | 17 | 116 | " | " | 4' 11" |
| Edna | 15 | 99 | " | " | 4' 10" |
| Mabel | 14 | 92 | " | " | 4' 8" |
| Lena | 12 | 90 | " | " | 4' 11" |
| John | 10 | 60 | Hazel | " | 4' 4" |
| Amanda | 45 | 135 | Brown | " | 4' 10" |
| Eli | 45 | 150 | Hazel | " | 5' 8" |

The following figures are beneath the chart:
35 3/4 # white, 42 3/4 # white, 2 3/4 # Brown
360 quarts to can 1942, 305 quarts canned June 1941

Following is Mother's Hospital Bill:    7-10-1946
C.C. Glass M.D.
Mr. Eli Yoder, Grantsville, Md., Hazel McGilvery Hospital
For professional services rendered and hospital @ $275.55

ITEMIZED:
6/26/46 Wife admitted to Hospital; 7/10/46 "" discharged

| | |
|---|---|
| 14 days in hosptal @ $6.00 | $84.00 |
| Operating room | 10.00 |
| Anesthetic fee | 10.00 |
| Laboratory fee | 4.00 |
| Routine Medication | 3.50 |
| Normal saline solution 1000cc | $2.50 |
| Dextrose 1000cc | 2.50 |
| Sulfa tabs. 35 @ .03 cents  1.05 | 6.05 |
| Board for special nurses 16 meals at 50 cents | 8.00 |
| Hospital | 125.55 |
| Operation and postoperative care in hospital | 150.00 |
| Total | $275.00 |

69

Hospital Bill February 16,1948
Admitted 2-3-48, Discharged 2-16-48
Itemized:

| | |
|---|---:|
| 14 Hospital days @ $6.00 | $84.00 |
| Operating room | 12.50 |
| Anesthetic | 12.50 |
| Lab. fee | 5.00 |
| Cumberland Lab. fee | 5.00 |
| Routine Medication | 2.10 |
| Special Medication | 15.09 |
| 22 Blood typings | 33.00 |
| 5 Blood Transfusions | 50.00 |
| Professional fee | 75.00 |
| | $294.00 |

Following is a list of men whose blood was typed and their types
Mother's was type 4- Eli Yoder 2, Henry 2, Paul 2, Ernest 2, Milt Beachy 2, Ervin
Beachy 2, Elmer Schrock 2, Olen Schrock 2, Norman L. Yoder 2, Menno L. Yoder
4, Eli Tice 2, Henry Tice 2, Jonas Tice 4, Monroe Tice 2, Lewis Tice 2, Vernon
Yoder 2, Menno Beachy 2, Alvin Beachy 2, Norman Beachy 2, Ervin Hershberger 2,
Simon Schrock 2.
Blood transfusions furnished: Philip Bender 1, Alvin Maust 1, Noah Yoder 1, Melvin
Beiler 1, Jonas Tice 1,

# Family Letter Sheets

Following are Dad's sheets from two Eli Yoder family letters:

June 29, 1970
Dear Children and Family.
  Well Lena thought I should write a sheet once for the family
and Paul said in his sheet of a spanking I gave him, when he
used the pencil on Henry's back. I do not remember now that I
ever gave any of the children a spanking more then with my big
mouth, and suppose that hurt about the same as a whipping. I do
not recall that I ever got a spanking from home. I remember I
thaught Dad and Mom were always good to us. Was I a good
boy or did I need a good spanking and dide'nt get it? I think that
was it. Dad said in his old days that if he had it to do over he
would raise his family, rather then to just leave them grow up.
So maybe if I was raised up and not just grown up I would have
been a better Dad to you. I know they were concerned about us ,
and think they done the best they knew how. We were always
taught to be obedient to the church and preachers and I want to
thank you children all that you have not caused us any trouble in
that which was and is a big blessing to us. Am only sorry I
wasn't a better dad to you and ask your forgiveness. Yes I know
you all did forgive me. Wish you all God's richest blessings.
  Only Dad

Mother started the following sheet and wrote about 10 lines with much effort. By this time Dad had also had some stroke problems for his writing is somewhat wavy and not like it was on the 1970 sheet:

Oct. 25, 1979 (3 and 1/2 years after her stroke)

Dear family circle,
Today 62 years ago we had our marriage vows and there was a deep snow but we went to church on wheels. I think sled would have been better but I think a lot of snow came down the night before. We had a lot of nice days after that. It does not seem that long at all. But time just rolls along. My parents had gone to Iowa that time, and then when they came back Eli and myself went to Norfolk and Delaware. (Now Dad took over) That was our honeymoon. We took the train in Meyersale to Washington and then we took a trolley to the boat landing and there we took a boat to Norfolk, and then a trolley out to the Amish and then from there we went to Delaware we crossed the bay on a boat and I think we went on train from there to Greenwood and was at Eighorns over night then went to Dover there were only a few families living there then at that time. then from Dover we went for home by train again. While we were at Norfolk we were invited to Simon D. Schrock and Sadie Yoder's wedding (Will's Sadie) and that was on Thanksgiven day. and now Simons are both gone a long time already and we are still here struggling around. Well we are so thankful that we can get around as good as we can. Amanda's right foot seems to be tightening up some which causes her more problem to walk, or to get started to walk. After she gets started I think it goes pretty good. Well we got rid of our guinea pigs and fish are gone and martin houses are cleaned, repaired and painted and and garden is finished so it seems I don't have hardly anything to do anymore. I will be making more Martin houses again. Well I am at the second one now for this fall. Well we are all in the Lord's hands, His will be done.
Dad and Mom

# Interesting Items From Sam Hershberger's 1895 TO 1898 Ledger
## (giving a glimpse of life in Mandy's childhood home)

Bought of S. Broadwater- 1. pair shoes $1.00, sandals .30 1. scissors .30, 3 silk handerchiefs .57
3 yds. flannel @ .25.... .75
Bought of U.M. Miller- Jan. 1896** 1 washing machine $3.00; 24 1/2 yards calico @ .05....$1.22; 2 blankets @ .25.. .50; 1 clock $3.25 total $8.22
Sept.18, 1896 Bought of H.Braodwater- 56 1/2 yds of mouslin @ .04....$2.26.
Bought of T. Bittinger 1 pk. toothpicks .05; 1 lb. crackers .05
Bought of H. Bros. 1 remnant .25; 2 yds. chambrac @ 12 1/2 .25; 2 yds. canton .08 .16; 5 yds. denim @ 12 1/2 .66; 1 remnant .25; 2 yds. calico @ 6 1/4 .13; 1 pr. shoes $1.00
Bought of Bes?? Co. 1 lunch .08

G.C. Keller by pulling tooth - $0.25

By dental work Charles Beachy - .50

Numerous entries of oats at .30 from J. J. Tice

Numerous entries of Medicines from S. J. Beachy    med. .95; linament .10; Powder
    .75

Bought of Cash buyers 1 Sewing Machine $16.50

J. D. Brenneman by 34 lbs. nails        .85

S. D. Yoder 1 ton fertilizer        22.50

Apr. 1897 Gehauff and Mayer 1 High Chair    1.00

E. Hershberger by fish 5 lbs. @.02 - .10; calf hide .01;, 3 1/4 lbs. bacon @ .08 -
    .26; 1200 lbs. hay - 7.20 also numerous entries for use of carriage .25 and
    one .95 for use of horse and .35 for use of carriage.

Bought of John Hetrick 1 dog $3.00

Nov. 1896, M. E. Hershberger by boiling applebutter $2.00

"    Bought of Eli Stanton        1 bbl. flour 4.40

"    "    " H. Bros. 17 yds. carpet @ .25 4.25

"    "    " Jack Stanton 6 cow chains @ .14 .84

"    "    " Joseph Shaw 100 lbs. sugar 5.00

Jan. 15, 1897 Dr. Lichti by work 8.00

(This was for delivering Amanda the mother of Eli Yoder's children).

There were also charges for medicines .15 to 25. Then Dr. Lichti bought 3 roosters
    at .20    .60  and 4 roosters for    .75

Bought of E. Hershberger 6 2/3 pecks pears @ .12 1/2 .84

"    "    "    "        5 gal. huckleberries @ .20 1.00

"    "    "    "        2 gal. raspberries    @ .20 .40

"    "    "    "        31 1/2 lbs. mutton @ .05 1.57

"    "    "    "        Liver .03

Frank Blucker by stable room and bed .25

J. Getty, 1 lamp- .25, 1 lantern- .50, 2 coal shovels- .25

Lee Cassort by making yarn 1.05

Oct. 1896 King Bro. Co. by threshing 11.75

Boarding of N.E. Hershberger by the day 1-29 to 3-20 2 meals @ .16 2/3, 3 meals
    @ .25, 1 meal @ .08 1/3

Subscription to paper .10

B. Miller 1 tooth brush .03

Misc. 1 yd. denim- .15; 1 yd. denim- .07; 1 bolt .01; 12 qt. strawberries @ .08 -
    .96; 1 pr. rubber boots 2.75

C.M. Livengood 1/2 pint WHISKEY .20

Rural New Yorker by advertising 6.30

Advertising in American Agriculturist 1.50

D.S. Beachy 1 wagon    71.84

E. Mulenberg 2 needles .02

J.S. Miller 11 lbs. soap grease @ .03 .33

N. Broadwater 2 quarts varnish

Bought of Rufus Beachy many bushels of coal @ .03 a bu. 22 1/2 bu. lime- $1.80; 1
    gal. turpentine- .55 save .55; 1 keg horse shoes- $3.17; Medicines from .10 to
    .15; nutmeg, pepper, allspice, ginger, cream of tarter, castor oil, prepaired
    camphor, Tincture of myrrh, corks and more ginger.


Sam Hershberger's employees & wages

Aug. 1896  Martin Winterburg by work 1 1/2 day $1.15

"    "    E. Hershberger  .50

72

Nov.     Katie Hershberger "   " .25
Sept.    Mrs. Winterburg  "   " 3.25
Nov.     W.    "     "   " 1/2 day .45
Misc. 1 yd. oil cloth .15, 1 hat .10, 1 pr. slippers .60

Cost of cellar
Pipe $11.73, Brick and tile $6.55, Cement $14.50; Charles Swauger's work $4.00;
    total $36.78

Sold to H. Bros. Co. 16 bu. apples @ .25 -$4.00; 2 bu. apples .30 .60; 150 lbs.
    grapes @ .02 1/2 -   $3.23
Sept.,1896 Sold to Mrs. Hanson 6 gal.apple butter @.50 3.00
"   "   "  " Wm. Yoder 100 lbs. beef @ .05 5.00
Sold to John Getty 22lbs. ham @ .10 2.20
"  "  "   "   16lbs. side meat @ .06 1/2 1.04
"  "  "   "   11 doz. eggs @ .12 1.32
sold in Frostburg   17 1/2 bu. apples 2.00
April 1897 sold to Simon Beachy  2 bottles wine .20
cabbage crop of 1899 mostly sold to Lamert @ .02
Moses Beachy .25, total crop  $121.24
1896 butter sold to H. Bros. Co. @ .20 a lb.

1903 Purchases
J.J. Bender 1 doz pr. socks .75, 4 yds. shirting .35
F.W. Bender 12 yds. pants stuff-$1.80, 10 yds. shirt stuff 1.30
1 Gal. paint $1.50, 1 looking glass .10, underwear .86
J.S. Miller 1 pear tree   .15

# Family Tree

1. Eli L. Yoder, son of Lewis S. and Elizabeth Beachy, Yoder was born May 27, 1896, died Jan. 5, 1983 married Oct. 25, 1917, in Niverton, Pa., to Amanda Hershberger, who was born Jan 15, 1897, and died May 29, 1983 daughter of Samuel and Elizabeth (Tice) Hershberger c. Elmer born Oct. 16, 1918 died Oct. 18, 1918, 2 Henry, 7 Paul, 14 Ernest, 22 Elizabeth, 30 Edna, 37 Mabel, 42 Lena, 49 John.

(Code - b.born, c.children, d.died, m.married, HM. home maker)

1976 Christmas. Seated: Amanda and Eli. Second row L-R: Lena, Mabel, Edna, Elizabeth. Back row: John, Ernest, Paul, Henry.

1970 Henry's family. Front L-R: Mary, Henry.
Standing L-R: Joseph, Sharon, Joanna, Moses.

2. Henry Yoder- was b. Nov. 9, 1919 and m. May 25, 1947 to Mary Elizabeth Beachy, b. July 15, 1920 dau. of Moses and Lucy Miller, (Beachy) in Niverton, Pa. c. 3 Joseph Ardon, 4 Eli Moses, 5 Rachel Sharon, 6 Joanna Ruth.
Ret. Yoder Meat Packers/HM.

R. 1, Box 125, Grantsville, MD 21536

3. Joseph Ardon Yoder was b. Apr. 16, 1948 and m. Aug.14, 1982 to Amanda Carolyn Miller b. Dec. 26, 1957 dau. of John and Mary Elizabeth (Beechy) Miller, in Burr Oak, Michigan. c. Jason Alexander b. July 24, 1985
Computer Systems Analyst/HM.

508 Walnut Ave., Scottdale, PA 15683

4. Eli Moses Yoder was b. Aug. 12, 1951 and m. Dec.20, 1980 to Karen Joy Miller b. Mar. 21, 1962, dau. of Edward and Melda (Tice) Miller in Salisbury, Pa. c. Patrick Nathaniel b. Sept. 28, 1982, Preston Daniel b. Aug. 22, 1984, Andrew Joseph b. Oct. 3, 1985, Anthony Moses b. Nov. 19, 1986, Amy Joy b. May 10, 1989, David Edward b. June 30, 1991.
Vice-President of Yoder Meat Packers/HM

R. 1, Box 187, Salisbury, PA 15558

5. Rachel Sharon Yoder was b. May 17, 1953 c. Jonathan Eugene b. Mar. 24, 1978
Teacher

Rt. 1, Box 132C, Catlett, VA 22019

6. Joanna Ruth Yoder was b. July 16, 1954 and m. May 26, 1979 in Salisbury, Pa. Glenn Howard Schrock b. Nov. 24, 1953, son of Herman and Elsie Yoder, Schrock
Farmer/HM.

R. 1, Box 183, Salisbury, PA 15558

1968 Paul Yoder family.
Front L-R: Marie holding
Marcella, Jesse, Sheldon,
Paul. Standing L-R: Ethel,
Michael, Nelson, Nathan.

7. Paul H. Yoder was b. Aug. 28, 1921 and m. July 5, 1953, Martha Marie Miller b. Apr. 24, 1925 dau. of Evan and Iva Maust, (Maust) in Grantsville, Md.  c. 8 Nathan Emerson, 9 Nelson Samuel, 10 Michael Evan, 11 Ethel Paula, Sheldon Mark b. Nov. 28, 1962 died April 5, 1992, 12 Jesse Conrad, 13 Marcella Joy
Minister, business partner/HM
(Ordained: Minister Sept. 1957 and Bishop Sept. 1975)

R. 1, B. 139, Grantsville, MD  21536

Note:  Sheldon Mark, fifth child of Paul and Marie, was born with Ataxia-Telangiectasia, a rare hereditary degenerative disease of the central nervous system, which caused progressive disabilities over the years. Though frail in body, Sheldon was strong in spirit and blessed with an enduring faith, keen mind, and a good sense of humor. He generally accepted his increasing physical limitations with unusual courage and dignity. Sheldon, having lived nine years beyond the life expectation of A-T patients, died April 5, 1992, at the age of 29 years.

8. Nathan Emerson Yoder was b. Aug.4, 1955 and m. Apr.14, 1979 in Goshen, Ind. to Miriam Grace Miller b. Sept. 7, 1955, dau. of John O. and Millie (Jones) Miller  c. Paul John b. Apr. 9, 1984, Amelia Marie b. Jan. 13, 1987, Evan Jay b. Dec. 6, 1989
Teacher/ LPN-HM

14713-1 S R 4, Goshen, IN  46526

9. Nelson Samuel Yoder was b. Dec. 23, 1956 and m. June 13, 1981 in Quakeertown, Pa. to Patricia Ann Shoemaker, b. Oct. 14, 1957, dau. of Richard Durrel and Lorraine (Alderfer) Shoemaker. c. Krista Renee b. Jan. 22, 1984, Kevin Darryl b. Sept. 5, 1986, Eric Brian b. May 5, 1989
Social worker/ nurse-HM.

5948 Michele Drive, Narvon, PA 17555

10. Michael Evan Yoder was b. Feb. 10, 1958 and m. Aug. 16, 1980 in Salisbury, Pa. to Delores Jane Schrock b. July 13, 1958, dau. of Olen and Miriam (Beachy) Schrock. c. Lisa Ranae b. Sept. 11, 1981, Angela Marie b. Apr. 25, 1986, Jessica Anne b. Aug. 16, 1990
Maintenance/HM.

R.1, B. 139B, Grantsville, MD 21536

11. Ethel Paula Yoder was b. June 23, 1960 and m. June 22, 1991 in Lancaster to Robert Gerald Zook b. June 28, 1964, son of Floyd and Elizabeth (Brubaker) Zook.
Teacher

2257 A Old Philadelphia Pike, Lancaster, PA

12. Jesse Conrad was b. June 7, 1964 and married Juanita Bixler June 18, 1988 b. March 29, 1967 dau. of Silas and Mary (Otto) Bixler. c. Ryan Jay b. Nov. 8, 1991

14261 Hackett Road, Apple Creek, OH 44606

13. Marcella Joy was b. Sept. 27, 1966
Student

Rosedale Bible School, Plain City, OH

1968 Ernest Yoder's family. Front L-R: Martha, Lena holding Regina, Ernest holding Joanna, Miriam. Standing L-R: Robert, Ruth, Marlene, Marlin.

14. Ernest Yoder was b. May 16, 1923 m Apr. 22, 1951 in Salisbury, Pa. to Lena J. Yoder b. July 15, 1931, dau. of Jacob S. and Fannie (Yoder) Yoder. c. 15 Robert Daniel, 16 Ruth Elaine, 17 Marlene Joy, 18 Miriam Louise, 19 Marlin James, 20 Martha Jane, 21 Joanna Grace, Regina Faith
Farmer/ HM

R.1, B. 21, Salisbury, PA 15558

Ernest drowned in their farm pond on his 63rd. birthday May 16, 1986.

15. Robert Daniel Yoder was b. Mar.18, 1953 m. Aug. 11, 1974 in Salisbury, Pa. to Ruth Elizabeth Kinsinger b.Aug. 4, 1954 dau. of Eli and Edna (Tice) Kinsinger c. Terry Lynn b. Dec. 10, 1976, Lyndon Eugene b. Jan. 22, 1978, Kevin Laverne March 3,1980
Trucker/ HM.

R. 1, B. 138, Grantsville, MD 21536

16. Ruth Elaine Yoder was b. Dec. 7, 1955 m. Apr.15, 1979 in Salisbury, Pa. m. Jerry Yoder b. Mar. 15, 1955 son of Crist and May (Yoder) c. Lori Donell b. Jan. 12, 1980, Nathan Lynn b. Dec. 20, 1981, Lorraine Yvette b. Mar. 26, 1983, La Nita Renee b. Dec. 29, 1986
Farmer/ HM.

R.1, B.35, Salisbury, PA 15558

17. Marlene Joy Yoder was b. Aug. 21, 1957 m. Oct. 24, 1981 in Salisbury, Pa. to Willis Sommers b. Dec. 10, 1956 son of John Sommers and Katie Beachy. c. Monica Joy b. Sept. 30, 1982, Melody Rose b. Dec. 9, 1983, Melissa Dawn b. Dec. 6, 1986, Wessley LaMar b. July 8, 1988, Melinda Fern b. Dec. 2, 1991
Mechanic in Beachy's shop/ HM.

R.1, B. 291, Salisbury, PA 15558

18. Miriam Louise Yoder was b. Apr. 21, 1963, m. Apr. 27, 1985 in Salisbury, Pa. to Reuben Sommers b. Sept. 30, 1962 son of John Sommers and Katie Beachy. c. Joel Ernest b. May 26, 1986, John Eric b. Feb. 8, 1988, Justin Laverne b. Jan. 31, 1990, Jared Wayne b. Aug. 12, 1991
Farmer/ HM

R.1, B. 21-A, Salisbury, PA 15558

19. Marlin James Yoder was b. Dec. 29, 1962 and married Gladys Guthrie Aug. 5, 1989 dau. of Robert and Elsie Guthrie.
Butcher

R.1, B.247, Grantsville, MD 21536

20. Martha Jane Yoder was b. May 20, 1964
House work

R.1, B. 21, Salisbury, PA 15558

21. Joanna Grace was b. Dec. 1967 and married Sept. 3, 1988 to James Kauffman b. Mar. 31, 1964 son of Joe and Tillie Kauffman. c. Jeffrey LaMar b. June 18, 1991

PO Box 48, Bittinger, MD 21552

1968 Ernest Beachey's family. Front L-R: Mary Jane, Elizabeth, Ernest, Anna. Standing L-R: Daniel, Naomi, Philip, Dorcas.

22. Elizabeth Yoder was b. Oct. 30, 1924 m. Oct. 21, 1945 in Salisbury, Pa. to Ernest N. Beachy b. July 22, 1920 son of Noah and Elizabeth (Tice) Beachy. c. 23 Daniel Moses, 25 Naomi Ruth, 26 Philip Glenn, 27 Dorcas Amanda, 28 Anna Marie, 29 Mary Jane
Machine Operator/HM

R.1 B. 184, Salisbury, PA 15558

23. Daniel Moses Beachy was b. Sept. 14, 1947 m. Apr. 19, 1969 in Catlett, Va. to Emma Byler b. Mar. 16, 1946 dau. of Norman W. and Mary (Beachy) Byler. c. Nathan Daniel b. Nov. 18, 1970, 24 Sharon Ruth, Timothy Andrew b. June 13, 1977, James Aaron, b. May 13, 1979
Director of Respiratory Therapy/HM

4640 Holley Ave., Fairfax, VA 22030

24. Sharon Ruth was b. Apr. 9, 1973 m. Feb. 22, 1992 to Michael Miller b. March 21, 1968 son of David and _____ Miller.
Farmer/HM

6105 TWP Road 419, Millersburg, OH 44654

25. Naomi Ruth Beachy was b. Oct. 10, 1949 m. May 18, 1974 in Salisbury,Pa. to Paul Nevin Petersheim b. Nov. 30, 1950, son of Henry and Elizabeth (Shetler) Petersheim. c. Matthew Duane b. Nov. 17, 1976, Rachel Dawn b. Aug. 30, 1978, Michael Shawn b. Dec. 25, 1979, Joshua Luke b. Jan. 16, 1982, Twins- Rebecca Anne - Deborah Lynne b. Nov. 29, 1983
Farmer/ HM.

R 1. B. 83, Oakland, MD 21550

26. Philip Glenn Beachy was b. May 27, 1952 m Oct. 4, 1975 in Salisbury, Pa. to Ruth Anne Zook b. Jan. 29, 1951 dau. of Yost M. and Amelia (Speicher) Zook. c. Anthony Philip b. July 26, 1977, Jenell Rose b. Jan. 2, 1979, Aimee Beth b. Sept. 27, 1980, Anita Joy b. Mar. 17, 1982, Rose, Marie b. Sept 6, 1985, Timothy Aaron b. Oct. 5, 1988
Farmer/ HM.

R. 1., B.184, Salisbury, PA 15558

27. Dorcas Amanda Beachy was b. Oct. 4, 1954 m. Apr. 10, 1976 in Salisbury, Pa., to Joseph M. Yoder b. Sept 8, 1951 son of Ervin E. and Saloma (Bontrager) Yoder. c. Amanda Jean b. May 29, 1983
Farmer/ HM

R. 1, B. 159, Grantsville, MD 21536

28. Anna Marie Beachy was b. Apr. 4, 1957 m. June 9, 1979 in Grantsville, Md. to Daniel Alvin Tice b. Aug. 10, 1956 son of Raymond and Ruth (Yoder) Tice c. Kendrick Jay b. Jan. 22, 1981, Carlita Faith b. March 31, 1982, Victoria Hope b. June 30, 1983, Lyndon Ray b. Aug. 21, 1986, Eric Jason b. Dec. 12, 1988
Farmer/ HM.

Box 984, Clayton, DE 19938

29. Mary Jane Beachy was b. Oct. 4, 1960 m. Sept. 27, 1980 in Salisbury, Pa. to William Ray Yoder b. Feb. 10, 1957 son of Noah E. and Sarah (Yoder) Yoder. c. Byron Quinn b. Aug 22, 1981, Brendon Eugene b. July 12, 1983, Douglas Lamar b. Dec. 7, 1985, Krista Joy b. Sept. 15, 1989
Farmer/ HM

R. 1, B. 252, Meyersdale, PA 15552

1963-4 Claude Beachy family. Front L-R: John Mark, Karla, Karen, Kristine, James. Back L-R: David, Edna, Claude.

30. Edna Yoder was b. Sept. 1, 1926 m. Jan. 1, 1949 in Salisbury, Pa. to Claude Raymond Beachy b. July 14, 1927 son of Joel and Annie (Hershberger) Beachy c. 31 John Mark, 32 James Conrad, 33 David Lynn, 34 Barbara Kristine, 35 Karen Ruth, 36 Karla Claudene Missionairies
(Claude ordained as minister 1954)

Radio H.C.J.B., Quito, Ecuador

31. John Mark Beachy was born Oct. 24, 1949 m. May 2, 1975 in Coaldale, Alta. to Florence Fay Baerg b. Oct. 10, 1955 dau. of Elmer and Martha (Heibert) Baerg. c. Marshall David Apr. 8, 1983, Ashley Dawn b. May 17, 1987
Computer Prog./HM.

9131 E. Shurwood Drive #623, Mercer Island, WA 98040

32. James Conrad Beachy was b. Aug. 6. 1951 m Apr. 14, 1973 in New Port News, Va. to Bonnie Jo Yoder b. Jan. 31, 1950 dau. of Morris H. and Janet (Weaver) Yoder. c. Elizabeth Erin b. July 24, 1977, Kristen Eve b. July 19, 1979
Computer Prog. and analyst/HM

Rt. 1, Box 5385, Paoli, IN 47454

33. David Lynn Beachy was b. Feb. 26, 1953 m. June 19, 1976 in Tiskilwa, Illinois to Marlene Kay Bachman b. Nov. 27, 1954, dau. of Allen David and Doris Alice (Schrock) Bachman. c. Emily Ruth b. Sept 28, 1982, Heidi Anne b. July 22, 1986, Katrina Louise b. Sept. 23, 1988
Doctor/HM

105 Elm Street, Paoli, IN 47454

34. Barbara Kristine Beachy was b. Jan. 4, 1958 m. Aug. 18, 1979 in Mt Pleasant, Pa. to Daniel Gehman b. Nov. 30, 1957 son of David Kay and Ellen Louise (Miller) Gehman c. Hans David b. Apr. 8, 1986, Katrina Michelle b. Sept 22, 1988
Elect. Engineer student/ HM

850 Detroit Ave., Morton, IL 61550

35. Karen Ruth Beachy was b. Sept. 30, 1960 m. May 4, 1985 to Mark Hartfield b. Aug 23, 1960. c. Roxanne Eve b. April 16, 1991 Director & teacher of Renaissance

618 Redmont Rd., Lebanon, PA 17042

36. Karla Claudene Beachy was born Dec. 1, 1961 married Nov. 5, 1988 to Ervan Litwiller b. Aug. 8, 1961. c. Joshua Ryan b. 2/6/92

213 S. Chestnut St., Tremont, IL 61568

1963 Raymond Schrock family. Front L-R: Marlin, Raymond, Mable, Wayne. Standing L-R: Ellen, Linda.

37. Mabel Yoder was b. Dec. 17, 1927 m. May 1, 1949 in Salisbury, Pa. to Raymond Schrock b. July 10, 1927, son of Elmer and Sadie (Hershberger) Schrock.c. 38 Ellen Marie, 39 Linda Ruth, 40 Wayne Edward, 41 Marlin James. Mabel d. of cancer July 21, 1987 Farmer/HM.

P.O. Box 119, Grantsville, MD 21536

38. Ellen Marie Schrock was b. June 17, 1950 m. Dec. 29, 1973, in Grantsville, Md. to Arnold Probst b. Feb. 3, 1951, son of Carl and June Probst. c. Keith Alan b. Sept. 10, 1976, Kenneth Arnold b. Feb. 15, 1979
Maint. wkr. at bank/bank wkr.HM

R. 1, B. 218 A, Williamsport, PA 17701

39. Linda Ruth Schrock was b. Oct. 28, 1953, m. May 6, 1972 in Grantsville, Md. to Paul Yoder b. Oct. 4, 1949, son of Noah and Sarah (Yoder) Yoder. c. Kevin LaVerne b. Jan. 25, 1975, Sherwin Dale b. Oct. 1, 1978, Bradley Wayne b. April 28, 1984, LaDawn Renee b. April 26, 1986
Carpenter/HM.

R. 1, B. 161, Hyndman, PA 15545

40. Wayne Edward Schrock was b. Aug. 13, 1957, m. June 23, 1984 in Grantsville, Md. to Felica Ann Harvey b. Dec 13, 1961, dau. of Joe and Judy Harvey. c. Lindsay Ann b. January 13, 1987, Darren Wayne b. Aug. 19, 1988, Kenton Mar b. April 24, 1990
Farmer/R.N. HM.

P.O. Box 180, Grantsville, MD 21536

41. Marlin James Schrock was b. Jan. 20 1960 m. May 16, 1981, in Bittinger, Md. to Norma Jean Bender b. Aug. 24, 1961, dau. of Elam and Mildred (Miller) Bender. Marlin died in a tragic accident Dec. 20, 1985.

Secretary

Accident, MD

1968 Elmer Beachy family. Front L-R: Kathy, Elmer, Lena, Brenda, Jason, Edith. Standing L-R: Rhoda, Esther, Edith.

42. Lena Yoder was b. Oct. 18, 1929 m. Aug. 29, 1952 in Salisbury, Pa. to Elmer Beachy b. Feb. 20, 1931, son of Noah M. and Elizabeth (Tice) Beachy. c. 43 Esther Louise, 44 Rhoda Joyce, 45 Orpha Grace, 46 Edith Irene, 47 Kathleen Ruth, 48 Brenda Jean, 49 Jason Edward
Feed dealer/ HM

R.1, B. 186, Salisbury, PA 15558

43. Esther Louise Beachy was b. July 16, 1955 m. Aug 6, 1977 in Grantsville, Md. to Leon Ray Hershebrger b. Dec. 17, 1954, son of Noah D. and Mary S. (Miller) Hershberger. c. Travis Dean b. June 18, 1978, Tiffiny Rae b. Aug. 6, 1980, Teresa Renae b. June 4, 1987
Feed delivery/HM

137 W. Henry, Wooster, OH 44691

44. Rhoda Joyce Beachy was b. May 19, 1957 m. July 24, 1976 in Grantsville, Md. to Dale Edward Curtis b. Mar. 15, 1953, son of Thomas Clayton and Betty Jean (Kelly) Curtis. c. Lisa Joy b. Sept. 17, 1978, Rebekah Jean b. May 12, 1980, Joel David b. Feb. 8, 1982, Jonathan Dale b. Feb. 20, 1984, Jesse Nathaniel b. Apr. 3, 1986, Joseph Allen b. Sept. 3, 1988
Chimney sweep, expert/HM.

P.O. Box 28, Grantsville MD 21536

45. Orpha Grace Beachy was b. May 28, 1959
Teacher

R.1, B. 186, Salisbury, PA 15558

46. Edith Irene Beachy was b. Nov. 4, 1961 married Aug. 6, 1988 to Thomas Miller b. Dec. 25, 1963 son of Melvin and Esther Miller  c. Christopher Thomas b. Dec. 9, 1989, Darryl Jay b. Nov.15, 1991 Computer/HM.

McConnellsville, OH

47. Kathleen Ruth Beachy was b. Jan. 27, 1964
House work

R.1, B. 186, Salisbury, PA 15558

48. Brenda Jean Beachy was b. July 26, 1965
Bakery Worker

R.1, B. 186, Salisbury, PA 15558

49. Jason Edward Beachy was b. April 23, 1968
Feed Bus. Delivery

R. 1, B. 186, Salisbury, PA 15558

1971 John Yoder family. L-R: Duane, Twila, Grace, John holding Sharon, Wendell.

50. John Yoder was b. Dec. 23, 1931 m. Apr. 18, 1957 in Salisbury, Pa. to Grace Yoder b. Apr. 18, 1937, dau. of Jacob and Fannie (Yoder) Yoder  c. 51 Duane Edgar, 52 Wendell James, 53 Sharon Dawn, 54 Twila Faye
Farmer/ HM

R. 1, B.320, Salisbury, PA  15558

51. Duane Edgar Yoder was born May 12, 1964 m. Sept. 25, 1982 in Grantsville,Md. to Sharon Ann Brown b. Oct. 15, 1959. c. Jennifer Marie b. Dec. 3, 1982, Shawn Duane b. Feb. 7, 1984
Trucker/ HM

R.1, B. 327, Salisbury, PA  15558

52. Wendell James was born Jan. 18, 1966

Salisbury, PA  15558

53. Sharon Dawn b. Oct. 30, 1967 married Aug. 18, 1990 to Ernest Stoltzfus b. Oct. 8, 1966 son of John O. and Lydia Stoltzfus
Route 1, Box 676, Honeybrook, PA  19344

54. Twila Fay b. May 7, 1970 m. Jan. 11, 1990, to James Hoover b. July 1, 1963. c. Cassandra Faye b. Oct. 20, 1990
Church St.,PO Box 35, Salisbury PA  15558

# Mother's Cookie Recipes

Ginger Cookies
3 1/2 cups brown sugar
2 cups lard
1/2 cup butter
3 eggs
1 1/2 cup Brer Rabbit green label molasses
1/2 cup hot water
1 teaspoon each of cinnamon, nutmeg and vanilla
3 teaspoons soda
3 tablespoons ginger
12 cups flour


Cocoa Drop Cookies
1 cup butter                    2 teaspoons vanilla
3 cups brown sugar              4 cups flour
2 eggs                          8 tablespoons cocoa
1 cup milk                      4 teaspoons baking powder

If you want to roll these, add more flour and chill the dough before rolling.


My Own Brown Sugar Cookies
10 cups soft brown sugar
5 1/2 cups lard- plus
1 teaspoon salt
2 teaspoons maple extract
3 teaspoons black walnut extract
5 cups whole milk sour or thick
10 eggs
10 tablespoons baking powder
6 1/2 pounds flour- (Pur-A-Snow)

Melt the Lard and mix with the sugar, then other ingredients and mix, about half of flour mixed with baking powder. I measure the milk and let it stand till it is sour.

Amanda

# Local Map

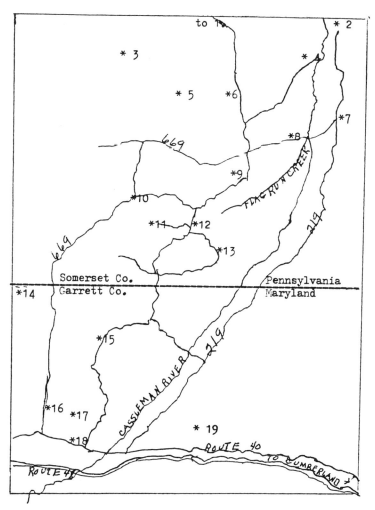

1. Mt. Davis, Pa.
2. Meyersdale, Pa.
3. Bennie Fisher Farm
4. Summit Mills Meeting House
5. Aaron Kinisinger Farm
6. St. Paul, Pa.
7. Salisbury, Pa.
8. Cross Roads School
9. Flag Run Meeting House
10. Springs, Pa.
11. Niverton, Pa.
12. Lewis Yoder Farm
13. Moses Beachy Farm
14. Posey Row Farm
15. Yoder School
16. Yoder Meat Packers
17. Sam Hershberger-
    Eli Yoder Farm
18. Grantsville, Md.
19. N.R. Davis - Marvin
    Kinsinger Farm